BRADSHAW'S GUIDES

Volume Four:
South Eastern Railways

Simon Jeffs

Series Editor John Christopher

AMBERLEY

About this book

This book is intended to encourage the reader
to explore many aspects of railway travel since
Bradshaw's times. Through his account and the
supportive images and information it describes
the history of the railways, their engineering
works, architecture and some of the many changes
that have occurred over the years. Hopefully
it will encourage you to delve a little deeper
when exploring the history of the railways, but
please note that public access and photography
is sometimes restricted for reasons of safety and
security.

Left: George Bradshaw. Although he died in 1853,
the guidebooks that bore his name continued
to be printed and will forever be known as
'Bradshaw's Guides'.

First published 2014

Amberley Publishing
The Hill, Stroud
Gloucestershire, GL5 4EP

www.amberley-books.com

Copyright © Simon Jeffs and John Christopher, 2014

The right of Simon Jeffs and John Christopher
to be identified as the Authors of this work
has been asserted in accordance with the
Copyrights, Designs and Patents Act 1988.

ISBN 978 1 4456 3416 6 (print)
ISBN 978 1 4456 3423 4 (ebook)

British Library Cataloguing in Publication Data.
A catalogue record for this book is available from
the British Library.

Typeset in 9.5pt on 12pt Celeste.
Typesetting by Amberley Publishing.
Printed in the UK.

Introduction

This is the fourth volume in this series of books based on *Bradshaw's Descriptive Railway Hand-Book of Great Britain and Ireland* which was originally published in 1863.

George Bradshaw was born in 1801 and died at the age of fifty-two in 1853. By chance he lived at a time of an unprecedented transport revolution. The railway engineers drove the iron roads, with their cuttings, embankments and tunnels, through a predominantly rural landscape to lay the foundations of the nineteenth-century industrial powerhouse that has shaped the way we live today. It is fair to say that the railways are the Victorians' greatest legacy to the twentieth and twenty-first centuries. They shrank space and time. Before their coming different parts of the country had existed in local time based on the position of the sun, with Bristol, for example, running ten minutes behind London. The Great Western Railway changed all that in 1840 when it applied synchronised railway time throughout its area. The presence of the railways defined the shape and development of many of our towns and cities, they altered the distribution of the population and forever changed the fundamental patterns of our lives. For many millions of Britons the daily business of where they live and work, and travel between the two, is defined by the network of iron rails laid down by the nineteenth century railway engineers and an anonymous army of railway navvies.

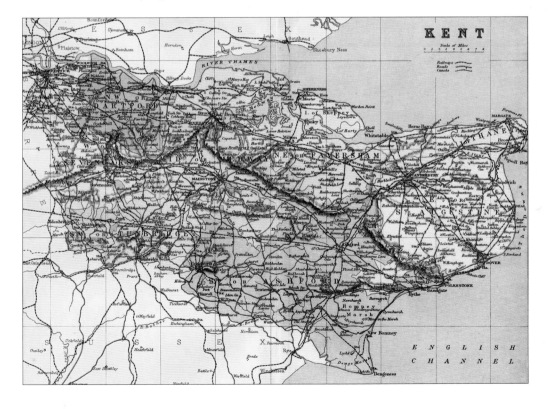

The timing of the publication of Bradshaw's guidebooks is interesting. This particular account is taken from the 1863 edition of the handbook although, for practical reasons, it must have been written slightly earlier, probably between 1860 and 1862. By this stage the railways had lost their pioneering status, and with the heady days of the railway mania of the 1840s over they were settling into the daily business of transporting people and goods. It was also by this time that rail travel had become sufficiently commonplace to create a market for Bradshaw's guides.

As a young man George Bradshaw had been apprenticed to an engraver in Manchester in 1820, and after a spell in Belfast he returned to Manchester to set up his own business as an engraver and printer specialising principally in maps. In October 1839 he produced the world's first compilation of railway timetables. Entitled *Bradshaw's Railway Time Tables and Assistant to Railway Travelling*, the slender cloth-bound volume sold for sixpence. By 1840 the title had changed to *Bradshaw's Railway Companion* and the price doubled to one shilling. It then evolved into a monthly publication with the price reduced to the original and more affordable sixpence.

Although George Bradshaw died in 1852 the company continued to produce the monthly guides and in 1863 it launched Bradshaw's *Descriptive Railway Hand-Book of Great Britain and Ireland* (which forms the basis of this series of books). It was originally published in four sections as proper guidebooks without any of the timetable information of the monthly publications. Universally referred to as *Bradshaw's Guide,* it is this guidebook that features in Michael Portillo's *Great British Railway Journeys,* and as a result of its exposure to a new audience the book found itself catapulted into the best-seller list almost 150 years after it was originally published.

Without a doubt the *Bradshaw guides* were invaluable in their time and they provide the modern-day reader with a fascinating insight into the mid-Victorian rail traveller's experience. In 1865 *Punch* had praised Bradshaw's publications, stating that 'seldom has the gigantic intellect of man been employed upon a work of greater utility'. Having said that, the usual facsimile editions available nowadays don't make especially easy reading with their columns of close-set type. There are scarcely any illustrations for a start, and attempts to trace linear journeys from A to B can be dfficult. That's where this volume comes into its own. This fourth volume of illustrated Bradshaw's Guides takes the traveller from London Bridge and Victoria stations via the former South Eastern Railway to the 'watering places' of the coast of Kent. Along the way the train calls in at a number of locations, including Greenwich, Woolwich, Gravesend, Rochester, Chatham, Margate, Broadstairs, Ramsgate, Deal, Dover and Folkstone. The various branch lines also take in Tunbridge Wells, Battle and Hastings as well as the cathedral city of Canterbury. The illustrations show scenes from Victorian times and they are juxtaposed with new photographs of the locations as they are today. The accompanying information provides greater background detail on the railways and the many locations along the route.

South Eastern Railway

By means of the South Eastern Railway (SER) the watering places on the coast of Kent, viz., Gravesend, Margate, Broadstairs, Ramsgate, Deal, Dover and Folkestone, can be reached in a few hours; and the inhabitants of the metropolis are thus enabled to enjoy the advantages of a visit to the sea-side at their favourite towns; the climate, temperature, and atmosphere of which many prefer and find more beneficial than that of the watering places on the south coast.

The London Terminus of the SER is situated on the Surrey or Southwark side of London Bridge. Its exterior view is not remarkable for architectural beauty or grandeur, although it is both large and convenient. From a comparatively insignificant terminus of the Greenwich line, it has been enlarged, and adapted to meet the requirements of the traffic of the various lines of which it is now the conjoint termini. The South Eastern Railway conveys to and from this terminus the passenger and goods traffic of a great portion of the county of Kent, and, via Dover and Calais, Folkstone and Boulogne, or Dover and Ostend, the passenger and goods traffic to and from France and the north of Europe. The London, Brighton & South Coast Railway (LBSCR) conveys the traffic of the counties of Surrey and Sussex, and also that with France, via Newhaven and Dieppe; and lastly, the passengers of the Sydenham Railway to and from the Crystal Palace.

The main or central building of the London Terminus belongs to, and is appropriated as the booking office of, the South Eastern and North Kent railways, the offices of the London & Greenwich being on the left towards Tooley Street. The right or south-western portion belongs to, and is appropriated as the booking offices of, the London and Brighton and Sydenham railways. On the left of the entrance there is an arcade, similar in some respects to the Lowther Arcade in the Strand, with shops, and a large refreshment room in the centre.

The interior of the station or terminus is admirably adapted for the traffic to these lines. The platforms are spacious and extensive; the wooden roofs over them are light and airy; and the plates of glass with which they are covered admit and diffuse sufficient light to every part of the vast area.

The arrangements appear so excellent that the trains receive or discharge their passengers from the respective lines simultaneously, without the least confusion being observed in any part of the united termini. Still one thing is wanting to render the complete, viz., the establishment of a Luggage Room, along the Parisian plan, into which all the baggage should be taken from the vans on the arrival of the trains, deposited on a counter, and delivered up only to the owner, upon his producing the respective duplicate ticket, and entrance to this room should alone be allowed to those persons who can produce that voucher. This would at once obviate the annoyance, delay, inconvenience, and risk which all travellers have to encounter, as regards that most necessary yet troublesome appendage, at all the stations in the kingdom, and prevent the possibility of any members of the 'swell mob', who attend every station, from profiting by the disorder, confusion, and scrambling which take place when traveller's

London Bridge Station

The station appears to have been almost continuously rebuilt since its formal opening as the terminus of the London & Greenwich Railway (as far as Deptford) in December 1836. Further rebuilds followed in 1839, with the arrival of the London & Croydon Railway, and in 1844, when the 'Joint' station, accommodating the London & Brighton and South Eastern Railways, opened. By 1861, after further enlargement and the addition of a large hotel, it had assumed the shape that Bradshaw's travellers would have known.

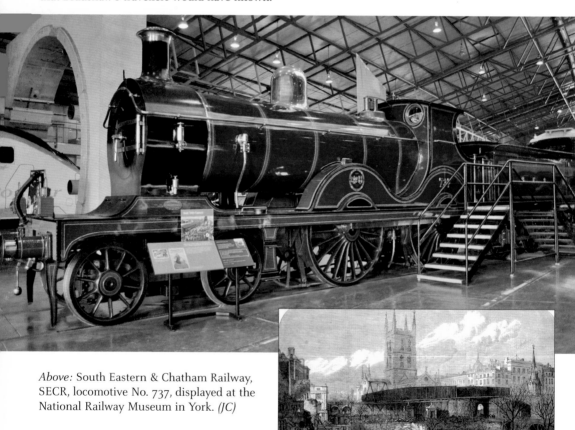

Above: South Eastern & Chatham Railway, SECR, locomotive No. 737, displayed at the National Railway Museum in York. *(JC)*

Right: This 1863 engraving depicts the extension to Charing Cross, then under construction, as illustrated.

luggage is unceremoniously flung down upon the platform at the stations for the owner himself to pick up.

The approach to the terminus from King William Street, over London Bridge, with its moving throng and exciting panoramic view – the ships and steamers of the river, the magnificent dome of St Paul's on the one hand, and the Monument on the other, with all the noble buildings encircling them, form one of the finest and most imposing views in London, or probably in the world – this extraordinary thoroughfare being a peculiar characteristic of the metropolis of England.

We commence our description of the Railway Routes in the county of Kent with the most northern.

Left: Currently (2014), London Bridge station is in the throes of redevelopment to accommodate an enhanced Thameslink service. When completed by 2018, there will be nine through and six terminating platforms. Overshadowed by the Shard, Networker 465242 waits to depart from Platform 6 with a Charing Cross train in October 2012 while the old train shed is prepared for demolition. (*Simon Jeffs*)

Above: Among other buildings to be pulled down are the South Eastern Railway offices in Tooley Street. The building is not listed and local efforts to have it preserved have been unsuccessful. (*'GB'*)

Deptford station is reputedly the oldest railway station in London and the oldest suburban station in the world on its original site, which dates from the opening of the London & Greenwich Railway in 1836. *Below:* On Deptford High Street, a former Class 421 (4 Cig) train carriage forms the heart of the Deptford Project and has become a local landmark. The carriage is currently stored elsewhere but should return once building work is completed. (*Simon Jeffs*)

Above: Passing on to Greenwich, the line crosses the Deptford Creek by a unique lifting bridge, now inactive. (*Simon Jeffs*)

The London & Greenwich Railway extension from Deptford opened on 29 December 1836. The handsome station building was designed by George Smith in 1840 and is still in use today, making it one of the oldest station buildings in the world. (*Simon Jeffs*)

Greenwich Branch, From London Bridge Terminus

Although this line has numerous competitors in the almost innumerable Thames steamers that ply between London and Greenwich, and the trips on board of which seem so much enjoyed by the pleasure-seeking crowds of London, the population of the great city is so immense that it pours forth its tributary streams in all possible directions over the bosom of the Thames whithersoever the steamers convey them, and into every corner of the country to which the railways from London will transport them. Hence, notwithstanding the competition of the steamers to and from Greenwich, there are as many as sixty trains daily by this railway to and from London. The line runs over viaducts the whole distance through the populous districts of Bermondsey and Rotherhithe, affording occasional glimpses of shipping on the river, until the train reaches

DEPTFORD

A telegraph station. HOTELS – Fountain; White Hart.

OMNIBUSES to London, New Cross, and Greenwich, every half hour daily.

POST HORSES, FLYS, etc., at the station and hotels.

DEPTFORD is a town in the county of Kent, built upon the banks of the Thames. The principal object of attention at Deptford is its dockyard, which has three building slips; but is chiefly used as a victualling yard, the river being crowded with transports. Evelyn, the author of *Sylvia*, had a seat here, which Peter the Great occupied when studying ship building. Sir F. Drake, after his famous voyage, entertained Queen Elizabeth on board the *Pelican*. There are also several private yards for the building of sailing vessels.

The General Steam Navigation Company's Engine and Boiler Manufactory and Dockyard, for their large fleet of steamers, is at the entrance of Deptford Creek, and is one of the most important and interesting establishments on the banks of the Thames. On quitting Deptford the train crosses the river Ravensbourne, and in a few moments reaches

GREENWICH

POPULATION, 139,436. A telegraph station.

HOTELS – Trafalgar, Charles Hart; the Ship Tavern, Thos. Quatermaine.

OMNIBUSES to and from London, Deptford, and New Cross, daily, every half hour.

STEAMERS to and from London, calling at all piers on the river, every five mins.

MONEY ORDER OFFICE, 12 Nelson Street. BANKERS – London and County Bank.

Greenwich Pier is five miles from London Bridge.

GREENWICH presents a striking appearance from the river, its Hospital forming one of the most prominent attractions of the place. Here was the palace erected by Humphrey Duke of Gloucester, and by him called Placentia; and here were born Henry VIII and his two daughters, Queens Mary and Elizabeth. Charles II began the magnificent present edifice, and William III appointed it to its present patriotic purpose, since which time

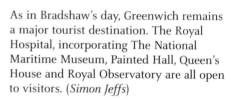

As in Bradshaw's day, Greenwich remains a major tourist destination. The Royal Hospital, incorporating The National Maritime Museum, Painted Hall, Queen's House and Royal Observatory are all open to visitors. (*Simon Jeffs*)

successive sovereigns have contributed to enrich it with various additions. As the first generally seen, we shall begin our description with an account of its interior.

The Chapel and Picture Gallery are open gratis on Mondays and Fridays; on other days threepence each is charged for admission. It is as well to remind the reader that the Hospital consists of four distinct piles of building, distinguished by the appellations of King Charles's, King William's, Queen Mary's, and Queen Anne's. King Charles's and Queen Anne's are those next to the river, and between them is the grand square, 270 feet wide, and the terrace, by the river front, 865 feet in length. Beyond the square are seen the Hall and Chapel, with their noble domes, and the two colonnades, which are backed by the eminence whereon the Observatory stands throned amid a grove of trees. In the centre of the great square is Rysbrach's statue of George II, carved out of white marble, from a block taken from the French by Sir George Rooke, and which weighed over eleven tons. On the west side is King Charles's building, erected chiefly of Portland stone, in the year 1684. The whole contains about 300 beds, distributed in thirteen beds, distributed in thirteen wards. Queen Anne's building on the east side of the square, corresponding with that on the opposite side, was begun in 1693, and completed in 1726. There are twenty-four wards with 437 beds, and several of the officers' apartments. To the south-west is King William's building, comprising the great hall, vestibule, and dome, erected between 1698 and 1703, by Sir Christopher Wren. It contains eleven wards and 554 beds. Queen Mary's building was, with the chapel, not completed till 1752. It contains thirteen wards and 1,100 beds. The Painted Hall, a noble structure opposite the chapel, is divided into three rooms, exhibiting, as you enter, statues of Nelson and Duncan, with twenty-eight pictures of various sizes; the chief are Turner's large pictures of 'The Battle of Trafalgar', the 'Relief of Gibralter', and the 'Defeat of the French Fleet under Compte de Grasse'. On the opposite side is Loutherbourg's picture of Lord Howe's victory on the memorable 1st of June, 1794, while above all are suspended the flags in battle. The other pictures up to the steps are chronologically arranged, the most prominent being the 'Death of Captain Cook', the 'Battle of Camperdown', 'Nelson leaping into the San Josef', and the 'Bombardment of Algiers'. It may not be generally known that every mariner, either in the Royal Navy or merchant service, pays sixpence a month towards the support of this noble institution, which has, of course, besides a handsome revenue (£130,000) derived from other sources. The pensioners, who are of every rank, from the admiral to the humblest sailor, are qualified for admission by being either maimed or disabled by age. Foreigners who have served two consecutive years in the British service are equally entitled to the privileges, and the widows of seamen are exclusively appointed nurses. The Hospital was first opened in January, 1705, and now the pensioners provided with food, clothes, lodging, and a small stipend for pocket money, number nearly 2,500. The number of out-pensioners is about 3,000. The Royal Naval School, for training the sons of seamen to the naval service, is a most interesting institution, administering the best instruction to now about 450 boys.

The Royal Observatory, occupying the most elevated spot in Greenwich Park, was built on the site of the old castle, the foundation stone being laid on the 10th of August 1675. The first superintendent of this establishment was Flamstead, and he commenced his observations in the following year. It stands about 300 feet above the level of the

Above: A link with maritime Greenwich is provided by the restored *Cutty Sark,* a British tea clipper built in 1869, representing one of the last and fastest sailing ships built before steam propulsion took over. (*Simon Jeffs*) *Below:* The Royal Naval School at Greenwich, *c.* 1900. The ship seen through the gates is a training ship and not the Cutty Sark which was taken into the dock at Greenwich in 1954. *(CMcC)*

river. For the guidance of the shipping the round globe at the summit drops precisely at 1.00 pm, to give the exact Greenwich time. The noble park is chiefly planted with elms and chestnut trees, and contains 188 acres. It was walled round with brick in the reign of James I. The views from the summit are very fine, embracing perhaps the finest prospects of London, and the Thames, the forests of Hainault and Epping, the heights of Hampstead, and a survey of Kent, Surrey and Essex, as far as the eye can reach. The flitting of the fawns through the distant glades, the venerable aspect of the trees themselves – many of them saplings in the time of Elizabeth – and the appearance of the veteran pensioners, some without a leg or an arm, others hobbling on from the infirmity of wounds or age, and all clad in the old fashioned blue coats and breeches, with cocked hats, give beauty and animation to a scene which no other country in the world can boast.

Around the side of the hill on a fair day or holiday are crowds of visitors in gay attire, some sitting on the grass discussing the contents of a friendly basket, while the junior members of the party are making the well-known coup-de-main of catching an unwilling maiden in their rapid and reckless descent, and then causing one of these general and irresistible shouts of laughter, denoting how much the discomfiture of the hapless damsel, promotes the fun and hilarity of the spectators, so that the joke is repeated over and over again with unfailing effect, and produces such a picture of joyous life and festivity, that even the 'Old Man of the Mountain' would relax his features to a smile, and perhaps be unable to control an indecorous ebullition of a hearty laugh.

A small doorway in the south-western extremity of the park brings us out with a sudden contrast on to Blackheath, where Wat Tyler assembled the Kentish rebels in the reign of Richard II, and where Jack Cade and his fellow insurgents are said to have held their midnight meetings in a cavern which still remains, though so choked up as to be considered nearly inaccessible.

On proceeding from the Park, towards Blackheath may be seen a group of emancipated youths eager and impatient to mount the donkey-steeds they have just hired, to take possession of and elicit the stubborn and wilful propensities of the race, or to display such feats of horsemanship as shall charm an admiring fair one in the surrounding groups, or more frequently to excite roars of laughter, witticisms and jokes, when the luckless rider is thrown, and exhibits that peculiar indescribable foolish appearance all persons, simple or gentle, manifest under similar circumstances.

Further on the visitor is certain to observe a dark eyed daughter of Bohemia examining the hand of some fair maid who has escaped from East Cheapside on a visit to far-famed Greenwich, to have her fortune told by one of the Gipsies of the heath. Ever and anon one of the ruder sex, facetiously sceptical, but evidently credulous in the occult art of the prophetess, wishes to look into futurity through the Gipsy Sybil, and then return to his avocations to wait the future fate she has predicted.

These are the principal objects of attraction and amusement in Greenwich and its beautiful Park which have diverted for centuries generation after generation of the good folks of London; and we cannot but hope that the Park and the Heath may be preserved for ages to come, as an oasis in the desert, when the mighty city has spread its suburbs far beyond it, into the hills and dales of the surrounding country.

North Kent Line

The North Kent line commences at NEW CROSS.

LEWISHAM (Junction)

A telegraph station. FAIRS – Horses, cattle and pigs, May 12th and October 13th.

LEWISHAM is a small village in a beautiful situation on the high road to Sevenoaks and Tumbridge, and near the river Ravensbourne.

BLACKHEATH

Distance from the station, ¼ mile. A telegraph station. HOTEL – Green Man.

The heath is celebrated for many remarkable events that have been witnessed on it in former periods of our history. The Danes encamped here while their fleet lay in the Thames a little above Woolwich. Wat Tyler and Jack Cade also encamped here with their followers, and since then the exploits of highwaymen and others have rendered the heath equally notorious. But it is now a favourite resort of the inhabitants of London, who come in crowds during the holidays and summer season – donkey riding being their favourite amusement. The heath is exceedingly picturesque, and commands several very fine views.

Lee and its church to the right.

From this station we pass through a tunnel 1,680 yards long, and arrive at

CHARLTON

Beckenham was once a small town in rural Kent, but since the arrival of the Mid-Kent Railway from Lewisham in what is now Beckenham Junction station in 1857, the town has grown massively and is now part of the London Borough of Bromley. Lines to Crystal Place and Shortlands followed in July 1858 and in 1863, the LC&DR extension to Victoria/Blackfriars completed the Victorian railway map. The original MKR building is still in use as the main Beckenham station offices and booking hall, and a branch of the Croydon Tramlink system now terminates here. *(Peter de Russett)*

A telegraph station.

CHARLTON is a small village, most pleasantly situated and remarkable for the numerous picturesque villas and residences it contains. From its being in the vicinity of Woolwich, and its charming neighbourhood, it is much frequented whenever a review or other military spectacle attracts visitors from town.

Pursuing our course we pass through two more tunnels, respectively 100 and 200 yards long, and arrive at WOOLWICH DOCK station, a short distance from which is WOOLWICH ARSENAL Station.

WOOLWICH

A telegraph station. HOTEL – Royal Pavilion.
STEAM BOATS from the pier to London every ¼ of an hour, calling at the
different piers on the river.
MARKET DAY – Friday. BANKERS – London and County.

Of course nearly all the interest connected with Woolwich is concentrated in the government establishments, which are acknowledged to be the finest in the world. These, consisting of the Dockyard, Arsenal and Royal Military Repository, we shall describe in the rotation generally adopted when seeing them. Coming from Shooter's Hill and crossing Woolwich Common, the extensive range of buildings forming the barracks of the Royal Artillery first attract attention. The principal front extends above 1,200 feet. In the eastern wing is the chapel, containing 1,000 sittings, and the other principal parts of the building are the library and reading-room, plentifully supplied with newspapers and periodicals. The whole establishment affords excellent accommodation for upwards of 4,000 men. The troops, when on parade, present a very animated appearance. The Royal Arsenal will be observed but a short distance off, composed of several buildings, wherein the manufacture of implements of warfare is carried on upon the most extensive scale.

On entering the gateway the visitor will see the Foundry before him, provided with everything necessary for casting the largest pieces of ordnance, for which, as in the other branches of manufacture, steam power has lately been applied. Connected with the Pattern Room, adjoining, will be noticed several of the illuminations and devices used in St James's Park to commemorate the peace of 1814. The Laboratory exhibits a busy scene, for here are made the cartridges, rockets, fireworks, and other chemical contrivances for warfare, which, though full of 'sound and fury', are far from being considered among the enemy as 'signifying nothing'. To the north are the storehouses, where are deposited out-fittings for 15,000 cavalry horses, and accoutrements for service. The area of the Arsenal contains no less than 24,000 pieces of ordnance, and 3,000,000 cannon balls piled up in huge pyramids. The Repository and Rotunda are on the margin of the Common, to the south of the town, and contain models of the most celebrated fortifications in Europe, with curiosities innumerable.

To the south-east of the Repository is the Royal Military Academy, for the education of the cadets in all the branches of artillery and engineering. The present building, partly in the Elizabethan style, was erected in 1805, and though 300 could be accommodated, the number

Blackheath

Once a favoured resort of Victorian Londoners, the Common at Blackheath is now ringed by housing and serves as a green space for locals.

Woolwich

Left: Historically, Woolwich was one of England's leading military and industrial towns, being home to the Woolwich Dockyard (founded 1512), the Royal Arsenal (founded 1671), the Royal Military Academy (1741) and the Royal Artillery (1716). The Arsenal finally closed in 1994, but an army base remains at the Royal Artillery Barracks. The Royal Artillery Museum, 'Firepower', is housed within the old Royal Arsenal (the original home of the regiment). The area became somewhat rundown since the closure of the Arsenal but has revived since the arrival of the DLR in 2009 at Woolwich Arsenal station. Some shooting events of the 2012 Olympic and Paralympics were held here, but photography within the town is currently difficult due to heightened security following a terrorist attack in 2013.

Middle left: Postcard of the Rotunda building at the Arsenal, *c.* 1904. *(CMcC)*

of cadets at present does not exceed 160. In going from the Arsenal to the Garrison there will be noticed, on the right of the road, an extensive building, forming the headquarters of the Royal Sappers and Miners. On the same side of the way is the Field Artillery Depot, where the guns are mounted and kept in readiness for instant action. The Hospital is to the left of the Garrison entrance, fitted up with 700 beds, and under the superintendence of the most skilful medical officers. From the Arsenal we proceed to the Dockyard, which, commencing at the village of New Charlton on the west, extends a mile along the banks of the river to the east. There are two large dry docks for the repair of vessels, and a spacious basin for receiving vessels of the largest size. The granite docks, and the Foundry and Boilermaker department, recently added, have been great improvements. Timber-sheds, mast-houses, storehouses and ranges of massive anchors, give a very busy aspect to the place, which was first formed in the reign of Henry VIII and considerably enlarged by Charles I. The new Royal Marine Barracks, designed by Mr Crew, and just finished, cost £100,000. An excellent feature is the kitchen, appropriated to every forty men, so that the meals may be taken apart from the bedroom. There is also a school attached for 200 boys and girls. The following form the arrangements of admission to the above important buildings: To the Arsenal, the Royal Repository, and the Dockyard, *free*; the hours being 9.00 till 11.00 a.m., and 1.00 till 4.00 p.m. Visitors are required to leave their names at the gates. The other buildings require the escort of one of the principal officers.

Though within the last four years nearly 2,000 additional houses have been built, the town presents few inducements for a prolonged visit, and has no feature of interest in itself whatever. The old church looks better at a distance than close, and there are a few monuments in the churchyard bearing names familiar to the eye and ear. Perhaps, after his visit to the Arsenal, the visitor will feel the most interest in that to Schalch, a Swiss, who died in 1776, at the advanced age of ninety years, sixty of which he passed as superintendent of the foundry there. Indeed, it was to him chiefly that the establishment owed its origin, for he was the cause of its removal from Moorfields, and the improvements made in conducting the operations.

From Woolwich we have the choice of four speedy modes of transit to town: first by steamer direct to London Bridge and Westminster; second by steam ferry across to Blackwall and so by railway to Fenchurch Street; third, by a similar conveyance to the new station of the Eastern Counties Railway, on the Essex bank of the river, which brings us to Shoreditch; and fourth, by the North Kent line. The excursionist may consult his own convenience for preference of choice. A delightful walk may be found over *Shooter's Hill* to *Elsham*, then by *Danson's Park* and *Welling*.

PLUMSTEAD Station.

Resuming our seat in the train, we proceed, skirting Plumstead marshes, the ordnance trial ground, to

ABBEY WOOD

Distance from station, 1 mile. A telegraph station.
OMNIBUSES to and from Bexley Heath. MONEY ORDER OFFICE at Woolwich.

Dartford is principally a commuter town and lies at the end of three lines from London (via Woolwich, Bexleyheath and Sidcup). As such, it is a major interchange and one of the busiest stations in the area, with over 3 million passengers a year. The station dates from 1849, but the buildings are of very recent construction, being completed in 2013. The EMU fleet used on the Dartford Lines is maintained at Slade Green Depot and mostly comprises the Class 465/466 Networker units. However, many commuters will remember the 'slam door' 4 EPB (Class 415) units, two of which (5001 and 5176) were repainted in green, and blue and grey livery in their final year of service. (*Brian Morrison*)

BELVEDERE station.

ERITH

Distance from station, 1 mile. A telegraph station.

OMNIBUSES to and from the trains; also to North Cray, Bexley and Crayford.

FAIR – Whit Monday. MONEY ORDER OFFICE at Dartford.

ERITH presents its picturesque church and wooded uplands to the right, and is a tempting village to loiter in when the opportunity serves. A fine pier, at which boats of the Diamond Company call, has been constructed for the accommodation of those who embark or disembark here, and an Arboretum, with extensive pleasure grounds, has recently been opened to attract visitors. Erith Church is a charming study for either artist or antiquary. The ivy which clings about the structure, and the masses of foliage that rise beyond, give it a very striking aspect. The structure consists of a nave and chancel, with a very low tower and spire, and evidently has a venerable length of years, for besides the date of some of the monuments going back as far as the year 1420, it has been identified as the spot where King John and the Barons drew up their treaty of peace. In the south chapel is an alabaster tomb, much mutilated, to the memory of Elizabeth, Countess of Shrewsbury, and her daughter Anne, Countess of Pembroke, who both died in the reign of Elizabeth. Adjacent are some fine brasses in good preservation, though the inscriptions attached to them have been quite obliterated. They all belong to the Waldens, members of the same family. *Belvedere*, the seat of Lord Saye and Sele, is an elegant mansion, in a very romantic situation, commanding extensive views over the country round. It was rebuilt towards the close of the last century, and contains some fine apartments of true aristocratic splendour. From Northumberland Heath, a spacious tract of fertile ground in this parish, the metropolitan markets are largely supplied with Kentish cherries, and in the neighbourhood some handsome houses and villas have been lately erected.

DARTFORD

POPULATION, 6,597. Distance from station, 1 mile. A telegraph station.

HOTEL – Bull. OMNIBUSES to and from the trains; also to Fremingham, via Sutton, twice daily. FAIR – August 2nd.

MONEY ORDER OFFICE. BANKERS – Hills, McRea & Co.

DARTFORD, built in a valley between two hills, derives its name from its situation on a ford of the River Darent. The insurrection of Wat Tyler originated in this town, and it has also been the scene of many other important events, the record of which would excite but little interest in the passing railway traveller. The trade is, however, considerable. It exports agricultural produce, and there are important gunpowder mills, corn and paper mills, establishments for calico and silk printing, and iron foundries in the neighbourhood. It has a large market, held on Saturdays. A large embattled gateway, and a stone wall enclosing 12 acres, are to be seen, the sole remains of its great nunnery, founded by Edward II in 1371.

Greenhithe/Northfleet

The area was once the site of many chalk quarries in one of which lies the Bluewater Shopping Centre. In addition, the high-speed London St Pancras International – Ashford–Cheriton (for the Channel Tunnel) – rail link bisects the area, with a station at Ebbsfleet from where trains depart to Ashford and East Kent and St Pancras International, both reached in a mere nineteen minutes. Several Eurostar services also call, heading for Brussels and Paris. Below: 10.42 Gravesend–Charing Cross at Northfleet station while 10.25 St Pancras International to Paris Nord is about to pass through Ebbsfleet, August 2008. (*'GB'*)

GREENHITHE

Distance from station, 1 mile. A telegraph station.
MONEY ORDER OFFICE at Gravesend.

Greenhithe Pier, 20 miles from London. *Ingress Abbey*, in the Gothic style, built with stones of old London Bridge. The chalk pits behind are pleasing. Gray's Pier, where Fidler's Reach and Northfleet Hope unite.

NORTHFLEET

Distance from station ¼ mile. A telegraph station. INN – The Leather Bottle.

On the London side of Northfleet, on the left of our line may be seen the beautiful asylum for decayed gentlemen, founded by the philanthropic brewer, Mr Huggins.

NORTHFLEET has an ancient church, one of the largest in Kent, containing several monuments of interesting antiquity, among which will be found one to Dr Brown, physician to Charles II, and some curious brasses of the fourteenth century. The extensive excavations about here, forming a sort of miniature Switzerland, not only give the scenery a wild and romantic aspect, but furnish valuable materials for the potteries.

The Rosherville Hotel, first class, family and commercial. Rosherville, though a suburb of Gravesend, belongs to the parish of Northfleet, and its neat pier is soon seen to the right, forming an elegant communication with that extensive range of buildings erected a few years since of the estate of the late Jeremiah Rosher.

GRAVESEND

POPULATION, 16,663. Telegraph station, No. 45, The Terrace.
HOTELS – The New Inn; the Terrace Hotel; the Clarendon.
OMNIBUSES at the station; also to Igntham (via Wrotham), Fairseat and
Meopham once daily. STEAM PACKETS to London, several times a day; to
Sheerness and Southend, daily, during the summer; to Tilbury, daily, every hour.
MARKET DAYS – Wednesday and Saturday. FAIRS – May 4th and October 24th.
BANKERS – London and County Bank.

GRAVESEND is one of the most pleasantly situated, and most easily attained, of all the places thronged upon the margin of the Thames. It is, moreover, a capital starting point for a series of excursions through the finest parts of Kent, and has, besides, in its own immediate neighbourhood, some tempting allurements to the summer excursionists in the way of attractive scenery and venerable buildings. The Terrace gardens, on each side the entrance to the pier, are really very creditably and tastefully laid out, and as a daily admission ticket can be had for twopence, expense is no obstacle to the public frequenting them. Directly you transverse the streets of Gravesend you see at a glance for what the town is famous. Shrimps and water-cresses tempt the visitor in every possible variety of supply, and places where both are obtainable, with 'Tea at 9*d* a head', are in wonderful numerical strength. Taverns and tea gardens are abundant, and most of them have mazes, archery grounds, and gipsy tents attached. There is an excellent

Gravesend/Cobham: The Dickens Connection
Gravesend is considerably eulogised by
Bradshaw and the town and its environs have
strong links to Charles Dickens who lived
in Gadshill Place, in Higham, not far from
Gravesend. *(Brian Morrison)*

In *David Copperfield*, Mr Peggotty, Ham
and the Micawbers say their goodbyes and
sail away from Gravesend to begin a new
life in Australia, while in *Great Expectations*,
Pip, with accomplices, rows Magwitch from
London down river to waylay a steamer
bound for Hamburg in the Lower Hope, off
Gravesend. A series of thirteen children's
graves, in the churchyard of St James in the
village of Cooling, on the Isle of Grain are said
to have inspired the opening scenes in *Great
Expectations,* and are popularly known as 'Pips
Graves.' *Right:* Charles Dickens. *(CMcC)*

MR. CHARLES DICKENS'S LAST READING.

market, held every Wednesday and Saturday; a Town Hall, built in 1836; a Literary Institution, with a Library, Billiard-rooms and Assembly Rooms inclusive, built in 1842; churches and chapels in abundance; numerous libraries and bazaars; water-works on the summit of Windmill Hill; baths by the river, and a commodious Custom House near the Terrace Gardens.

Windmill Hill is, however, the magnet of the multitude, and is crowned by an excellent tavern, The Belle Vue, to the proprietor of which belongs the old windmill – the first erected in England and as old in its foundations as the days of Edward III. Here, refreshments are provided on the most liberal scale, and an admirable camera, together with some pleasure grounds and a labyrinth of ingenious construction, offer the best and most captivating allurements to visitors. The moderate outlay of one penny entitles the visitor to a telescopic view from the gallery, where the horizon forms the only limit to the vision. There is, on a fine day, a magnificent prospect of the river Thames, as it winds towards the Nore, a distinct survey of the counties of Kent and Essex, and even glimpses of the more distant ones of Surrey and Sussex, including the most noted eminences in each. The shipping at the Nore can be clearly distinguished, although 36 miles distant; Southend in Essex, Hadleigh Castle, the village church at Leigh, a place renowned for its shrimp and oyster fisheries, the isles of Sheppey, Grain, and Calvey are all visible to the east; north and north-west are the Laindon Hills on the opposite shore, farther westward Highgate and Hampstead Hills, with a portion of Epping Forest; south-west, Shooter's Hill, with its commemorative castle of Severndroog, appears rising from a woody undulation; Knockholt Beeches, verging on the very borders of Sussex; and nearer to the hill the sequestered villages of Swanscombe. Looking in a more southerly direction, and beyond the fertile parishes of Wroxham, Ifield, Singlewell, and Meopham, the extensive plantations and sylvan glades of Cobham Park rise on the left, surrounding the ancient hall of the old Lords of Cobham, and now the property of the Earl of Darnley; while immediately beneath the eye of the spectator ranges over the unbroken line of picturesque buildings that comprise Rosherville, Gravesend and Milton, with (on the opposite coast) Tilbury Fort and its extensive moat, the Ferry-house, the villages of East and West Tilbury, Stanford-le-Hope, Horndon, Shadwell, East and West Thurrock, and a castellated mansion called Belmont. The fertile valley, seen from this height, looks like a Brobdignag estate on a Lilliputian scale; the smoke seems to stand still in the air, the reapers in the field look like Dutch-clock automata, while the cattle that here and there dot the plain appear as if some holiday Miss has emptied out the contents of Noah's Ark. The hedges shrink to rows of boxwood, and the gigantic oaks dwindle to diminutive shrubs.

But of all the places round, none shall neglect an excursion to COBHAM, four miles distant, where, in the old wood and hall, a day's enjoyment can be most fully insured. There are several vehicles always ready to be hired, that will take the visitor by reasonable rate by road, but as those who can appreciate a delightful walk will not find the distance too fatiguing, we shall indicate the route for the pedestrian. Taking the footpath at the back of Windmill Hill, the pedestrian will find it traversing a picturesque country, now crossing the sweeping undulation of a corn field, and anon skirting a shaded copse, with bluebells and primroses starting up in prodigal luxuriance through

Back in Gravesend town, the station was completely rebuilt in January 2014. The images show the 1849 South Eastern Railway station in 1853; still in use in 2013 with a Class 395 unit on a special service from St Pancras International to Ramsgate passing in January 2009; and after its very recently rebuilt form in January 2014. *(SER Guide, Brian Morrison, David Rowlands)*

the tangled underwood. We next pass through a hop plantation, and in summer when the bine has swung up to the top of the poles, and the shoots have thrust themselves off to the next, and so joined in a leafy communion of luxuriant vegetation, the scene becomes truly Arcadian, and an excellent substitute for the vineyards of the south. Leaving the little village of Singlewell to the right, we have a finger-post to guide us, and a few minutes after reach the outskirts of this sequestered village. The first object to which the visitor will naturally direct his attention is the old church, occupying rising ground in nearly the centre of the parish, and having on the southern side an extensive view. The antiquarian may here enjoy a great treat in inspecting the ancient monuments to be found in the interior, as there are several brasses of the Cobham family, successive generations of which, from the year 1354, have lived and died in the parish. On the altar-monument, in the middle of the chancel, are two full length effigies, with several children around them in a kneeling position. This was erected to the memory of George Lord Cobham, who had been the governor of Calais in the reign of Elizabeth, and who died in 1558. On the tomb of Maud de Cobham is a curious sculptured figure of a dog, and one similar will be found in the chancel on the tomb of Joan, wife of Reginald Brybroke. They are worthy of notice, as exemplifying the attachment felt towards two faithful canine adherents to the fortunes of the family. Outside, on the southern wall, there are some elegant tablets too, of the Darnley family. In 1714, the Hall and estate came by marriage into the possession of an Irish family of the name of Bligh, one of whom, in 1725, was created Earl of Darnley, and the seat of the Earls of Darnley it has continued to be ever since. The Hall is a massive and stately structure, consisting of two wings and a noble centre, the work of Inigo Jones. The oldest portions are those at the two extremities, flanked with octagonal towers. The Picture Gallery, having a choice collection of paintings by the old masters, and the unique gilt hall, form the most prominent features of attraction in the interior, but the apartments besides are elegantly furnished, and the quadrangle and old brick passages of the outbuildings wear about them an aspect of unmistakable antiquity. On the south side, leading up to the principal entrance, is a noble lime tree avenue, extending upwards of 3,000 feet in length. In the park, which is nearly seven miles round, there are some noble oak and chestnut trees, many of them measuring 20 feet and upwards in circumference. It also has the reputation of producing venison of superior flavour, derived from peculiar excellence of the herbage, and it was on this fare probably that both Queen Elizabeth and Charles II were regaled when they visited Cobham; for the former, according to Styrpe, was welcomed with a 'delectable banquet and great cheer'. In a romantic spot, towards the south-east end of the park, on an eminence called William's Hill, there is a spacious mausoleum, erected in 1783, by the present Lord Darnley's grandfather. It is built of Portland stone, in an octagonal form, after the Doric order and cost £9,000, but never having been consecrated, it has not been devoted to the purpose for which it was intended.

Cobham Wood is a glorious region for the rambler, and the footpath to Rochester, through the very heart of its sylvan solitudes, a delightful track to follow. The pedestrian can also return, through the wood, Upper Shorne, and Gad's Hill where Prince Hal and his eleven men in buckram robbed Jack Falstaff, to Gravesend by way of Chalk. Either way a day's enjoyment is complete.

The first station from Gravesend is

HIGHAM

A telegraph station.
Gad's Hill (1 mile); *Cliffe* (3 miles); *Cowling* with its castle (3¼ mile) – an embattled gateway forming a picturesque object.

From Higham we pass through a tunnel, 1¼ mile long, under Higham Down, a chalky ridge. Emerging from which we arrive at

STROOD

A telegraph station. HOTEL – Old George. STEAM BOATS to Sheerness daily.

A bridge over the Medway, replacing the old bridge built in the reign of Rufus, recently demolished, joins this town with

Rochester

At the lowest bridging point of the River Medway, Rochester is famed for its castle, cathedral, Kings School (dating from AD604 – the second oldest school in England), associations with Charles Dickens (who based many of his novels in the area), Sweeps and Dickens Festivals, it is now a major tourist destination. Until 1998, it was part of Kent but now, with Chatham, Gillingham and Strood, it makes up the Medway unitary authority area.

Descriptions of the town appear in Charles Dickens's *Pickwick Papers, shown left, Great Expectations* and as 'Cloisterham' in *The Mystery of Edwin Drood.* Miss Havisham's (from *Great Expectations*) house, Satis House, was based on Restoration House in Crow Lane, left. *(Laurel Arnison, Simon Jeffs)*

ROCHESTER

Distance from the station, ½ mile. Telegraph station at Strood, ½ mile.

HOTELS – Victoria and Bull Inns; Crown.

STEAM BOATS to and from Sheerness, twice daily.

SAILING VESSELS (hoys) to and from London, twice weekly.

MARKET DAYS – Friday and Saturday; 4th Tuesday in each month for cattle; every Tuesday for corn.

FAIRS – May 15th, 19th; September, each three days. August 26th, 27th and 28th.

At Rochester, which has a population of 16,862 and returns two members, some projecting gable houses are to be seen in the High Street, with an old town hall, built 1687; Sir C. Shovel's clock-house; Watt's almshouse for poor travellers, 'not being rogues or proctors'; Henry VIII's grammar school; and St Nicholas Church, built 1421.

It is an ancient borough town in the county of Kent, having been a British town before the Roman invasion, and stands in a rich vale on the banks of the Medway, on an angle of land formed by that river. On the east it is connected by a continued range of buildings with the town of Chatham, and on the west by the village of Strood. The three places form almost a continuous line of houses, and are often collectively called the 'Three Towns'.

The Cathedral has a half-ruinous look outside, but contains some excellent Norman work, especially the west door and the nave, lately restored by Cottingham; the pinnacled tower, 186 feet high, is of later date. Total length, 306 feet, with a double transept – one 122 feet, the other 90 feet long. With the exception of the west front and the great tower, the exterior of the cathedral is destitute of ornament; its plain massive walls presenting a remarkable contrast to the highly decorated and varied appearance of its great rival at Canterbury. There are effigies of bishops, including Gundulph, and the founder of Merton College, Oxford; service at 10½ a.m. And 3¼ p.m. on weekdays. Close at hand are remains of a chapter-house, cloister, etc.

The Castle of Rochester, of more remote origin than the cathedral itself, attracts the notice of the traveller by its venerable and majestic appearance – magnificent even in ruins. It stands on a rock over the river, and is 70 feet square and 102 feet high, in four stories, with turrets at the corners, like the Tower of London, of which Bishop Gundulph was also the founder. Much civility is shown to visitors. A galley runs all round the keep, and seats are placed at intervals here and there in the different stories, to afford views of the splendid prospects that keep breaking upon the sight in all directions with increased extent and grandeur as you wind round and round to the top, whence the whole panorama is exposed to view without interruption; admission, daily (Sundays excepted), 3d each. The Medway, at high water, here appears a fine broad stream between green sloping banks.

An amphitheatre of hills encircles the beautiful landscape. The Medway below serpentines round the castle, and then the cathedral and the bridge. Rochester consists principally of one long street called High Street, which crosses it from east to west, terminating on the river a little below the new iron bridge.

In the vicinity are Upnor Castle, a fort built by Queen Elizabeth to guard the town (1½ miles); Cobham Park and Hall (3 miles); Gad's Hill (2½ miles); and Blue Bell Down

The South Eastern Railway and London, Chatham & Dover Railway built bridges across the Medway to Rochester, the latter conveying the SER's branch from Strood to Chatham while the former took the LCDR's London–Dover main line into the Medway towns from 1861. The SER had its own station in Rochester, Rochester Common, plus a second in Chatham, Chatham Central. Both closed in 1911 and all services now call at the LCDR station, Rochester. However, from 1927 the Medway rail bridge has been that of the SER while the piles of the LCDR structure were used for the second road bridge, opened in 1970 (see map of Rochester area). Network Rail intends to build a new station at Rochester 500m east of the current facility. *('GB')*

After the First World War, Chatham Dockyard became a major centre for submarine building. HMS *Ocelot* forms a centrepiece of the museum. With the establishment of Army barracks and forts which provided a defensive shield for the dockyard, Chatham's population grew rapidly and it is now the major town within the Medway conurbation. The dockyard closed in 1984, but has been redeveloped as a major tourist attraction, the Chatham Historic Dockyard. *(Simon Jeffs)*

on the Maidstone road, a walk over which, crossing over Aylesford Bridge, and back by the banks of the river, will be found interesting and alluring.

CHATHAM

Distance from station, 2 miles. A telegraph station.

HOTELS – The Sun; the Mitre. STEAM BOATS to and from Sheerness, twice daily.

MARKET DAY – Saturday. FAIRS – May 15th, Sept. 19th (each for three days).

A parliamentary borough, returning one member, but best known for its naval dockyard, on a bend of the Medway, 19 miles from the Nore, and about 2 miles from the Strood terminus of the North Kent Railway. Omnibuses run through Rochester to meet every train, and the Sheerness steamer touches here. Population, 36,177, including 7,000 or 8,000 dockyard-men and soldiers. Depots of the marines, of several regiments of the line, and East India service, are stationed at Chatham. It was a fishing village in Saxon times. In the disgraceful reign of Charles II, the Dutch Admiral De Ruyter came up so far as to burn the ships and carry off the Royal Charles.

After passing through a tunnel of 1¼ miles, under Higham Down, a chalk ridge is seen stretching out into the river opposite Chatham. Rochester and Chatham form one straggling dirty town, hemmed in by chalk downs, which, on the Chatham side, rise up rather steeply to a very considerable height. There are the 'Lines', which are strengthened by Fort Pitt, Fort Clarence and other military works. They should be ascended for the extensive view of the towns, the Medway and the Thames, they offer, etc. Chatham is here seen stuck like a wedge in a gap of the downs. The *Dockyard* (to be seen by application at the gate) was commenced by Queen Elizabeth, following the wise policy of her father, and is about a mile long. It contains six building slips, wet and dry docks, *Rope House*, 1,140 feet long, blacksmith's shops, steam sawmills, oar and *block machinery* by [Marc] Brunel, a duplicate of that at Portsmouth, copper sheathing and paint mills, pattern room, arsenal, etc. Several ships in ordinary are moored in the river. A ship-gun battery and school are attached to the

MARINE BARRACKS – These are barracks also for the Royal Engineers and Sappers and Miners, with a school for young officers and recruits, where practical lectures are given upon everything relating to the art of war. Good libraries for both services, and naval and military hospitals. Here Drake and Hawkins founded the *Chatham Chest*, or fund for the benefit of seamen. In the parish church (which replaces one mentioned in Domesday Book), is the monument to *Stephen Burroughs*, the first Englishman who, with Willoughby, sailed by the north-east passage to Russia.

SHEERNESS, at the Medway's mouth, is another naval dockyard, in a dull, flat part of the Isle of Sheppey, near the Nore. Fossils are abundant in this island. Sailors say that 'at Plymouth it always rains, at Portsmouth it always blows' but at Sheerness it always rains and blows', which may give an idea of the delightful climate prevailing here.

POPULATION, 8,549.

Chatham station dates from 1858, serving the North Kent and Dover main lines, and is squeezed into a valley between Fort Pitt and Chatham Tunnels. Enthusiasts can enjoy an industrial railway within the dockyard, which operates a variety of steam and diesel heritage traction. This view shows Navy divers in action at a Chatham Navy Week in the 1930s. *(CMcC)*

Above left: The Isle of Sheppey is connected to the mainland by the Kingsferry Bridge, which is a combined road and railway vertical-lift bridge and was opened in 1960. *('GB')*

Above right: Sheerness is the largest town on the Isle of Sheppey (Island of Sheep) and began life as a fort built in the sixteenth century to protect the River Medway from naval invasion. By 1669, a Royal Navy dockyard was established in the town, where warships were stocked and repaired until its closure in 1960. Although Sheppey has some pretensions as a resort, it remains primarily an industrial centre and active port, developing into a major steelmaking centre. Unfortunately, the steelworks closed in 2012, which dramatically impacted upon the island's economy. Sheerness was connected the LCDR main line by a branch from Sittingbourne, the station dating from 1860. *(Simon Jeffs)*

LONDON, CHATHAM & DOVER

Victoria to Chatham and Dover

When completed, this company will have two termini in London, the one from Victoria at the West End, the other from Farringdon Street in the East, where it will unite with the Metropolitan or Underground Railway. The Eastern or Metropolitan extension section of the line joins with that of the Western at Herne Hill, but is in an unfinished state beyond the ELEPHANT and CASTLE, to and from which station passengers are now booked. This portion of the line passes by CAMBERWELL and CAMBERWELL NEW ROAD to the junction. The Western terminus is at Victoria, from whence trains run via the stations of STEWART'S LANE, WANDSWORTH ROAD, CLAPHAM and BRIXTON to

HERNE HILL, from whence we proceed over a viaduct of thirty arches, 1,000 feet in extent, and which has from a distance a very picturesque appearance. Beyond this is an embankment of a mile and a quarter, in the middle of which is Dulwich station. Following the embankment is a cutting of one third of a mile in extent, with slopes of 4:1. This brings us when at the depth of 60 feet, to the tunnel under Sydenham hill, and at the face of which there is now being erected a station for the accommodation of the neighbourhood. Immediately beyond the tunnel, the line passes under nine lines of railway belonging to the South Eastern and Brighton Companies. We next come to a small cutting which brings us to

PENGE, and an embankment, similar in character to the one already mentioned, brings us to BECKENHAM. We next pass the station of SHORTLANDS, and at the distance of a mile further arrive at

BROMLEY

A telegraph station. POPULATION, 5,505.

Principally composed of one long street; market house, supported on pillars. Dr Johnson's wife and Hawkesworth, the author of the *Adventurer*, lie buried here.

BICKLEY and ST MARY'S CRAY stations.

SEVENOAKS JUNCTION – A line here turns off to the right, 8 miles long, passing through EYNESFORD and SHOREHAM, to

SEVENOAKS

A town of some importance, deriving its name from that of its founder, Sir W. Sevenocke.

FARNINGHAM – Lullingstone and Eyneford Castles in the neighbourhood.

MEOPHAM and SOLE STREET are then passed; and at a distance of six miles beyond, the arrival of the train is announced at STROOD (the North Kent junction), which, together with ROCHESTER and CHATHAM, have been described.

NEW BROMPTON station.

RAINHAM (a telegraph station).

One of the villages on the Old Roman road, Watling Street, passing which, and the station of Newington, we arrive at that of

SITTINGBOURNE (a telegraph station)

Near to which is the old town of 'Milton', situated on a creek or arm of the Swale, in which the celebrated 'Milton Natives' are dredged. The town was a demesne of the Saxon kings. In the struggle with King Alfred, the Danes had a camp here, the remains of which, popularly called Castle Rough, yet exist. In the centre of the town there is an ancient court house. The church is large and handsome, with an embattled tower, chiefly in the decorated English style.

MARKET DAY – Saturday. Much corn is shipped here.

SITTINGBOURNE & SHEERNESS

A branch 7 miles long turns off to the left at this place, running direct across the western extremity of the Isle of Sheppey, passing through QUENNBOROUGH, to SHEERNESS, described previously.

Continuing on the Chatham and Dover route:

Herne Hill was provided with a handsome station by the LCDR in 1862. In 2014, the exterior has hardly altered and the building is now Grade II listed and notes the station's arched doorways, Welsh slate roof and decorative brickwork. *(Graham Feakins)*

TEYNHAM (a telegraph station)

In the vicinity of which are *Rodmersham Lodge* (2 miles); *Teynham Lodge* (2½ miles); *Norton Court* (2 miles); and arrive at

FAVERSHAM

POPULATION, 5,858. A telegraph station.

MARKET DAYS – Wednesday and Friday. FAIRS – October 11, 12, 13.

This town is situated on a small stream running into the East Swale, which is navigable for vessels of 150 tons. It was a place of much note before the time of Stephen, who, however, built and endowed an abbey here for the Cluniac monks, and in which himself, his queen, and his son Eustace were buried. At the dissolution, Stephen's remains were thrown into the river, for the sake of the leaden coffin in which they were contained. Some portions of the outer wall still exist. The church is cruciform, and built of flint, in the decorated style; the tower and spire (a copy of St Dunstan's in the East, in London), are of modern date. The Market House was erected in 1594. There is a well-endowed Grammar School. Here James II was held prisoner on his attempt to escape from England. There are some imports and a considerable coasting trade, which necessitates the establishment of a Custom House. Gunpowder is a branch of Manufacture.

Near the town is *Davington*, where there was a nunnery founded by *Fulke de Newnham*, in 1153, the sister's house and the church still remaining. Near *Ospringe* (1 mile) is Judd's Hill, the Roman *Dunolevum*, close to which is *Tindal House*; *Ospringe House* (1 mile); *Monte Video House* (1 mile); *Lees Court* (3 miles) the seat of Lord Sondes; *Belmont* (3 miles), Lord Harris; and *Nash Court* (3¼ miles).

Whitstable Branch

This branch turns to the left, taking a direction coastwise by the Whitstable Flats to WHITSTABLE. A distance of 3¾ miles further brings us to

HERNE BAY

Distance from Sturry station, 6 miles. A telegraph station.

HOTELS – Pier and Dolphin. OMNIBUSES – to and from Sturry station, three daily.

MARKET DAY – Saturday. FAIR – Easter Monday.

HERNE BAY, so named from the old village of Herne, about a mile and a half distant, which was thus called from the number of herons frequenting the coast at this point, was not twenty years ago more than a scanty collection of houses, irregularly built along the beach. It has now become a fashionable and somewhat populous watering-place, with long lines of streets, many of them still unfinished, stretching out in every direction. In 1831, a pier from one of Telford's designs was commenced, and now presents an elegant and substantial structure, extending 3,640 feet over the sands and the sea. At the extremity are commodious flights of steps for the convenience of small vessels and passengers landing at low water, and a fine parade sixty feet in width and upwards

Left and middle: Bromley is first recorded in a charter of 862 as 'Bromleag', meaning 'woodland clearing where broom grows'. There would be very little space for woodland or broom now in this bustling town, which has become the commercial centre of the largest borough in south-east London, with a population of over 300,000. The first station, now Bromley South (since 1899), opened in 1858 and has been extended as the town grew. The line through the station was quadrupled in 1893 and the present station on the overbridge provided, giving access to two long island platforms. *(Peter de Russett)*

Below left and bottom: Bradshaw provides scant information about Sevenoaks as the branch from Swanley Junction to the town had only opened the year before, on 2 June 1862. Indeed, so quiet was the area that the station was named 'Bat and Ball', after a local pub. On 2 March 1868, a second station, known as 'Tubs Hill', was opened in the town on the route of the SER's St Johns–Tonbridge cut-off line to Dover. This is now the principle station and is used by over 4 million passengers a year. It also provides access to Knole House, home of the Sackville family since the thirteenth century. Contrary to popular belief, the 'seven oaks' were not planted at Knole until 1902 and six of them were lost in the Great Storm of 1987. *(Peter de Russett, Simon Jeffs)*

Sittingbourne

A transport centre since Roman days, located midway between London and Dover, where Watling Street meets the sea. Once the railways arrived in 1858, Sittingbourne changed from a market and coaching town to a brick and paper-making centre, using the abundant clay and chalk reserves in the area. Indeed, the bricks for the London & Greenwich Railway viaduct were made in Sittingbourne, then shipped by barge down the Thames. Paper manufacture at Kemsley Paper Mill still continues today and a reminder of the industrial railways that once served this industry is provided by the preserved Sittingbourne & Kemsley Light Railway. The station, like so many in Kent, primarily conveys commuters to London, but also serves as the interchange for the branch to Sheerness. *('GB', Peter de Russett, Simon Jeffs)*

Faversham was established as a settlement before the Roman conquest and, like its neighbour Sittingbourne, became a Roman town complete with large amphitheatre. Saxon kings resided there and the abbey, established in 1148, became the final resting place of its founder, King Stephen. It is the centre of the English hop-growing industry and the Shepherd Neame Brewery, founded in 1698 and claimed to be the oldest in the country, still makes beer in the town. The company sponsors annual steam-hauled railway excursions. *(Laurel Arnison)*

The cradle of the UK explosives industry, Faversham was the scene of a terrible explosion of TNT in 1916, killing 105 – the worst accident of its kind in Britain. Over 2 million rail journeys aremade from the station, which is the terminating point of high-speed services from St Pancras International and where many services between London Victoria and East Kent divide and join to serve Canterbury/Dover and the Isle of Thanet resorts. The station has a profusion of Victorian ironwork and retains its Grade II 1898 building. Well worth a visit, if only to sample the local beer. *(Peter de Russett)*

of a mile in length has been formed on the adjoining shore. The air is very bleak but invigorating, and the sea purer, it is considered, than at Margate. A considerable portion of the adjacent land, and the very side of the town itself, was anciently covered by the waves, constituting the estuary which admitted the passage of large vessels, and divided the Isle of Thanet from the mainland. Mrs Thwaites, the widow of a wealthy London merchant, has proved a munificent benefactress to the town, for, in addition to having built and endowed two large charity schools, she has caused to be constructed also a clock tower, which serves the purpose of a lighthouse as well. A new church has been built in the centre of the town, with a chapel of ease and a dissenting chapel, and there is also an infirmary for boys from the Duke of York's military school at Chelsea. On the Parade is a large bathing establishment, with an elegant assembly room adjoining, to which apartments for billiards, reading, etc., are attached. Libraries and bazaars have recently been introduced in the usual number and variety. The old village church, with its embattled roof and square tower, is a spacious edifice, comprising a nave, two aisles and three chancels.

Resuming our journey along the main line, a distance of 6½ miles beyond the station of SELLING brings us to the archiepiscopal city of CANTERBURY, described later.

A distance of 15 miles brings us through the little villages of BEKESBOURNE, ADISHAM (the station for Wingham), SHEPHERD'S WELL and EWELL to Dover.

South Eastern continued – MAIDSTONE BRANCH.

Strood to Maidstone

On leaving Strood, the line, skirting the banks of the swift Medway, soon bring us to

CUXTON, or CUCKSTONE

A telegraph station.

This place contains a population of 384, who are engaged in the hop trade, beautiful crops of which are yearly obtained from this neighbourhood. The old church is an antique edifice, and contains some pews as old as the time of the Reformation. In the vicinity are the villages of Luddesdown, the church of which contains a tomb to the lords of the manor, the Montacutes; Meopham, with its ancient church, rebuilt in 1333 by Archbishop Meopham, a native; and *Meopham Bank*, the pretty seat of W. N. Smith Esq., and *Wouldham*. Proceeding through a magnificent hop country we arrive at

SNODLAND

A telegraph station.

In the vicinity are *Burham* and *Byrling*, in the church of which are buried many of the Sayes and Nevilles, to whom there are brasses. The farm called Cornfort and Birling Place, with its gate and ruins, were their seats. On the banks of the Medway near, are the Episcopal ruins of *Halling*.

Cuxton/Snodland/Aylesford

In the 1860s, the top end of the Medway valley between Strood and Maidstone West was predominantly devoted to agriculture, particularly for growing hops. Now it has become heavily industrialised and residential, with the Medway town conurbation impinging on the north and Maidstone to the south. Slicing through the centre, between Cuxton and Strood, is the high-speed line (HS1) between London St Pancras International, Ebbsfleet, Ashford and the Channel Tunnel, crossing the Medway on a spectacular viaduct. *(Simon Jeffs)*

Many of the stations on the Medway Valley line were provided with imposing station buildings, visible in the images of Snodland and Cuxton, but are now unstaffed and suffer from vandalism and neglect.

Above: Cuxton.

Right: Snodland. *(Ashley Saunders)*

38

Soon after leaving Snodland the train crosses the Medway, and we arrive at

AYLESFORD

A telegraph station.

The ancient *Aegelesford*, has a population of 1,487, employed in the hop gardens. Here the Saxons under Hengist and Horsa were defeated by the Britons under Vortimer, A.D. 455, but Catigern, his brother was killed, and to whose memory is said to have been erected the remarkable cromlech, popularly called *Kit's Coty House*, still to be seen one mile north-east from the village. In the year 1016 the Danes were pursued hither by Edmund Ironside. There is an excellent Free Grammar School. The Church, beautifully situated on an eminence, is an ancient foundation, and contains brasses of the Colepeppers, Rycants and Sedleys (the Poet of Charles II was of this family, and resided here). Close to the Medway to the west are the remains of the Carmelite Friary, founded by Lord Grey of Codnor, in 1240, made habitable by restorations and additions at various times, and now the seat of the Earl of Aylesford. The celebrated traveller, Rycant, was born here, 1628. In the vicinity are *Boxley Abbey* (1¾ miles) Lady Finch, and *West Malling* (3 miles) with the remains of its Benedictine Nunnery, a beautiful specimen of Norman architecture. At St Leonard's, a tower 71 feet high, the remains of its ancient chapel. *Bradbourne House* (2 miles). *Allington* (2 miles), with its old castle, which was the seat of Sir Thomas Wyatt, the scholar of Henry VIII's day, and his son, who suffered for treason against Queen Mary. *Preston Hall* (1 mile).

South Eastern Main Line

This has been called the 'Pleasure Line'; and certainly the beauty and extent of the country traversed by its trains justly entitle it to that distinguishing appellation. It is not only the great medium of daily communication between London and Paris, or England and the Continent, but its iron roads and branches intersect the beautiful county of Kent in all directions, affording the inhabitants of the great metropolis facilities of visiting

Aylesford has a very long history. In AD 455, the Saxons under Hengist and Horsa were defeated here by the Britons under Vortmier. Vortmier's brother, Catigern, is popularly believed to be buried under the cromlech known as 'Kit's Coty House' near the village but this structure, one of the first in England to become a scheduled monument, is probably the remains of a Neolithic chambered long barrow, one of six in the Medway district. *(Simon Jeffs)*

Redhill

A major junction between the north-south London–Brighton line and east-west Reading–Tonbridge line, once part of the SER's main route to Dover and the Continent. The name derives from the red sandstone through which the Tonbridge branch was constructed and the LBSCR's 'Quarry Line', avoiding Redhill, was tunnelled in 1899. Platform 3 of the station retains many buildings from the 1858 rebuild. *(John Scrace, Simon Jeffs)*

Almost immediately after the London & Brighton reached Redhill, plans proliferated for lines to the west, with the Reading, Guildford & Reigate Railway (RGRR) company succeeding in 1846 and opening throughout by 1849. Despite shareholder opposition, the line was purchased by the SER in 1852 and has always struggled financially, being converted to 'Paytrain' operation, with most of the minor stations left unmanned, from 1965. Reigate is the only manned station between Redhill and Reigate and retains a direct service to London for its heavy commuter traffic, the line being electrified in July 1932. *(Colin Scott-Morton)*

the numerous watering places on its coast, and enabling them to become acquainted with its picturesque scenery, cities, and baronial halls, and the astonishing fertility of its soil.

London to Reigate

No sooner is the train in motion than we escape from the confinement of the station and emerge into purer air – although the first mile we pass over no less than a dozen streets, thronged with a restless, busy population, who inhabit the dense neighbourhood of Horsleydown and Bermondsey.

The Greenwich Railway diverges to the east, and to the west is the branch to the Bricklayers' Arms, built upon arches, and extending by the side of the Surrey Canal over a long tract of market-garden ground.

With a distant glimpse of the wood-crowned heights of Greenwich, and a near view of a large red-brick building – The Royal Naval School – we arrive at the great locomotive station of the Brighton and Dover companies; the Nunhead Cemetery, about a mile to the right. A range of undulating eminences beyond Peckham and Dulwich, rapidly pass into view, and a few miles further on, almost before the eye can take in the range of the picturesque suburban scenery, we reach New Cross.

From New Cross the train diverges from the North Kent line, and proceeds through a deep cutting that conceals all the view of the country, to the Dartmouth Arms Station at Forest Hill, an exceedingly pretty spot, which is becoming a favourite residence of an increasing number of families from the metropolis. A mile beyond is the Sydenham station, in the midst of very lovely scenery, and in view of the fairy-like scene of the Crystal Palace, with its marvellous transepts, wings and galleries, situated in the most exquisite and park-like grounds – ornamented with a noble terrace, commanding one of the finest views in England, and embellished with waterfalls, cascades, and splendid fountains – all on such a vast and magnificent scale as to suggest the idea of it being the palace of the Celestial Empire of China, rather than that of the people of England – by whom it ought to be liberally supported. At a short distance beyond Sydenham the line leaves the border of Kent and diverges more into the county of Surrey. The Anerley station, although in a pretty situation, deserves no particular mention, in comparison with the celebrated one of Norwood.

A short distance beyond Caterham Junction the railway enters the celebrated Merstham Tunnel, which is said to have cost £112,000. Emerging thence the train reaches the village of

MERSTHAM

Distance from station, ¼ mile. A telegraph station.

MAILS – One arrival and departure, daily, between London and Merstham.

Merstham is situated to the right of the line – formerly famous for its apple orchards. There are valuable stone quarries in the vicinity. The old church on the hill contains

Merstham

In Bradshaw's day, this was the main line to Dover and the Continent as the SER's cut-off between St Johns and Tonbridge was not opened to passengers until May 1868. Quarries at Mertsham were served from around 1805 by the Croydon, Merstham & Godstone Iron Railway (CMGIR), a branch of the world's oldest public railway, the Surrey Iron Railway. When the London & Brighton Railway was building its line towards Redhill, it was obliged to purchase the moribund CMGIR, which it paralleled between Croydon and Merstham in 1838. Some relics of the GMGIR are on display within Barons Cave at Reigate. Merstham station is reached by a 1,820-yard tunnel and very deep cutting through the North Downs which is currently undergoing massive repair works. *(Peter Burgess, Network Rail)*

An extensive series of line quarries were located to the north of Betchworth station, served by a network of narrow gauge railways of 3-foot 2¼-inch gauge. One steam and one diesel engine from this system survive at the Amberley Chalkpits Museum. *(Simon Jeffs)*

some curious monuments and tombs. The seat of Sir W. G. H. Joliffe, Bart., MP, is a noble looking mansion.

After this the line enters the Great Junction Station at

REIGATE (Red Hill)

A telegraph station. HOTEL – Railway Hotel. MONEY ORDER OFFICE at Reigate.

This is one of the most important junctions of the Kent and Sussex railways. The *London & Brighton Railway* diverges from the station southward, through Sussex. The Reigate and Reading branch goes to the west, through the vale of Dorking to Guildford and Reading, communicating thence to any part of the kingdom.

On alighting at this station the traveller will find himself in the midst of the celebrated valley of Holmesdale, surrounded on all sides by elevated hills. To the north appears the great chalk range, bearing a rugged and abrupt front, broken into precipitous cliffs, or crowned with undulating heights. To the south is seen the sandstone ridge, with the celebrated mount of coloured stone, known as the Red Hill.

REIGATE TOWN

POPULATION, 9,975. Distance from station, ½ mile.

A telegraph station. HOTELS – White Hart, and Swan.

POST HORSES, FLYS, etc., at the station and hotels.

MARKET DAYS – Tuesdays. FAIRS – Whit-Monday and December 9th.

MONEY ORDER OFFICE.

BANKERS – London and County Joint Stock Banking Company.

REIGATE, situated near the River Mole, in the valley of Holmesdale, at the foot of the ridge of chalk hills which traverse the country from east to west, consists of a main street of well-built houses, crossed at the eastern end by the Old Brighton Road, which, for upwards of a mile out of town, is adorned by the detached residences of the gentry. The houses of the lower classes present models of architecture, and are beautifully decorated with imbricated tiles of various patterns, a style of cottage ornament characteristic of this part of the country. The church stands on a gentle eminence east of the town, and is a spacious structure of almost every period of Gothic architecture, some parts of which are extremely beautiful. From the summit of Park Hill an extensive view is obtained of the wealds of Surrey and Sussex; and that of Reigate, with the priory and its park, is of singular beauty. On the north side of the town, in the principal street, was situated the castle, some few traces of which are yet visible. It was one of the principal seats of the powerful Earls of Warwick and Surrey; and here the insurgent barons are reported to have held frequent meetings, preceding the celebrated Congress of Runnymede. There is a long passage under the castle mound leading into a vaulted room, called the Baron's Cave, which is said to have been used by the barons as a hiding-place for arms. The church has a few curious and ancient tombs.

Reading, Guildford And Reigate Branch

Reigate to Reading

This line connects the county towns of Berkshire and Surrey (Reading and Guildford), and extends from the latter across the garden of Surrey to Reigate; at the same time communicating with four trunk lines – the Great Western, the South Western, the Brighton, and the South Eastern Railway. To the pleasure tourist we scarcely know any presenting so many picturesque attractions. Its route lies from Reading along the South Eastern line, across Berkshire, by Wokingham and Sandhurst, entering Surrey by Tinley; then crossing the South Western line, onward with a branch to Farnham; at the base of Hog's Back to Guildford; next by a branch to Godalming, and continuing at the foot of the celebrated range of chalk hills past Dorking and Reigate to Red Hill. We have alluded to the picturesqueness of the Surrey portion, which will be new ground to many a tourist; though it is perhaps, the most beautiful scenery of its class in England. Its landscapes present a quick succession of 'morceaux' for the painter in its uplands, woodland, dells, verdant valleys, rocky hills and undulating parks and heaths, all lying within the eye of the traveller along this line. Betchworth Park is among the most beautiful specimens of this scenery between Reigate and Dorking, although the part of the chalk hills seen from that point is greatly exceeded by the bolder sublimity

Boxhill/Dorking

Renamed Deepdene in 1923, to avoid confusion with Box Hill and Westhumble station on the Horsham–Sutton line and Dorking (Deepdene) in May 1987, this is the principle station on the Reading–Redhill line in Dorking and, despite its minimal facilities, is very busy with commuting schoolchildren. The SER tried to promote it as the railhead for Box Hill. *(Michael Fife)*

of Box Hill, the venerable giant of the chain, with its luxuriant clothing of patronymic evergreen.

As a pleasure line, this portion is very popular, passing as it does through an exceedingly fine country, with the scenery of which excursion trains have already made thousands of visitors familiar.

BETCHWORTH

A telegraph station.

Within a short distance, situated most beautifully in a romantic park washed by the 'Sullen Mole', are the ruins of *Betchworth Castle*. They are most picturesque, and the grey walls, contrasting with the rich green of the ivy creeping over a great part of them, stand out finely against the deep blue sky.

Proceeding on our way, with the lofty down on our right, we pass over the Mole by a viaduct 50 feet high, and then through Box Tunnel to the station at

BOX HILL

A telegraph station.

Tourists alight at this station for the hill with its celebrated prospects. It took its name from the Box trees planted thereon in the reign of Charles I and is now a resort for picnic parties. This is the nearest station likewise for *Mickleham*, a charming village, 2¼ miles distant.

HOTELS – Running Horse, Fox and Hounds.

Norbury Park (2½ miles), H. P. Spirling, Esq. A beautiful seat surrounded by fine plantations. One mile beyond this is the town of *Leatherhead*.

DORKING

POPULATION, 4,161. Distance from the station, ½ mile.

A telegraph station. HOTELS – Red Lion, and White Horse.

OMNIBUSES to and from the station; to Epsom station several times daily;

to Brighton and London thrice weekly.

MARKET DAY – Thursday. FAIR – The day before Holy Thursday.

MONEY ORDER OFFICE.

BANKERS – London and County Joint Stock Banking Company.

DORKING is situated in a valley near the river Mole, nearly surrounded with hills, and commands some of the finest views in the kingdom. This town is of considerable antiquity, and so conveniently situated that it carries on a large trade in flour and corn, and employs several mills on the Mole. The church is a fine old edifice and contains several handsome monuments. It is celebrated for its poultry, particularly for a five-toed breed, called Dorkings, supposed to have been introduced by the Romans. It is a favourite summer resort of invalids and lovers of rural scenery, and it would be difficult to name any place better calculated for both classes, as the salubrity of the air and the

Guildford

This is the county town of Surrey, home to a castle, the University of Surrey and an Anglican cathedral. It is of Saxon origin, probably located where the River Wey was forded by the Harrow Way. On the building of the Wey Navigation and Basingstoke Canal, Guildford was connected to a network of waterways that aided its prosperity. The station was opened by the London & South Western Railway (LSWR) on 5 May 1845, but was substantially enlarged and rebuilt in 1880. The RGRR arrived on 4 July 1849, while services to Farnham in October 1849; to Horsham in October 1865; and the New Guildford Line to Leatherhead and Epsom Downs in February 1885; completed the railway map. Although modernised by British Rail, the station is a rather untidy, unattractive affair and could do with a complete rebuild. *(Simon Jeffs)*

Wokingham means 'Wocca's people's home' after a local Saxon chieftain, becoming a market town from 1219. From the fourteenth to the sixteenth centuries, Wokingham was well known for its bell foundry which supplied many churches across the south of England, while during the Tudor period, Wokingham was well known as a producer of silk. It is said that one of the original mulberry bushes (favourite food of the silk worm) still remains in one of the gardens of Rose Street. The formerly important industry of brick-making has given way to software development, light engineering and service industries and the inevitable London commuting. The RGRR line from Reading arrived on 4 July 1849, followed by the Staines, Wokingham & Woking Junction Railway (SW&WJR) on 9 July 1856. The LSWR worked the SW&WJR and was authorised to run over the SER to Reading, thus giving Wokingham a direct route to London Waterloo. A completely rebuilt new station has very recently (2013) opened – a great improvement over the dreadful British Rail 1973 CLASP structure. *(Stuart Hicks)*

beauty of the surrounding country cannot be surpassed or equalled within so short a distance of the metropolis. There are several very beautiful country-seats, villas, and mansions around the town, too numerous, however, to be enumerated in our pages.

The line, still skirting the Downs, soon brings us to the station of

GOMSHALL and SHEIRE

A telegraph station.

Sheire was the residence of Bray, the antiquarian, who edited Evelyn's *Memoirs*. In the immediate vicinity is *Abinger Hall* (2 miles), the seat of Lord Abinger. *Netley Place* (1½ miles). *Albury Park* (1½ miles). Near which is Newland's Corner, from which a most extensive prospect may be obtained.

East Horsley (3 miles). *Ewhurst* (5 miles).

CHILWORTH

Distance from the station, 1 mile. A telegraph station.

On an eminence in the vicinity, and towards the south, is St Martha's ancient chapel. *Chilworth Manor* is the property of Godwin Austin, Esq. About two miles further on is

SHALFORD

POPULATION, 8,020. A telegraph station. HOTELS – White Lion and White Hart. OMNIBUSES to and from the station. POST HORSES, FLYS, etc., at the stations and hotels. MARKET DAYS – Saturdays, Tuesday and Wednesday. FAIRS – May 4th and November 22nd. MONEY ORDER OFFICE.

GUILDFORD

POPULATION, 8,200. A Telegraph station. HOTELS – White Lion and White Hart. OMNIBUSES to and from the station. MONEY ORDER OFFICE.

The situation of this town on the banks of the Wey, and spreading over the steep hill as it rises from the side of the river, is particularly picturesque. It consists of a principal street, nearly a mile long from the bridge on the west to Stoke on the east, whence several smaller streets extend into the suburbs.

Guildford Castle is supposed to have been built as early as the time of the Anglo-Saxon kings. The principal part now remaining is the keep, of a quadrangular form, rising to the height of 70 feet, and built on an artificial mound of earth. Admission may be had free on application to the proprietor of a school adjoining the castle grounds.

Two miles to the eastward of the town is a fine circular racecourse. The roads in the neighbourhood are extremely picturesque – that from Guildford to Farnham in particular, running along a ridge of high chalk hills, and thus commanding an extensive prospect. The trade of the town is considerable, from its central situation and convenient distance from the metropolis. The guild or town-hall and the corn market are handsome buildings.

ASH

Distance from the station, ¼ mile. A telegraph station.

OMNIBUSES to and from the station; also to the Farnham station.

MONEY ORDER OFFICE at Farnham.

The line now diverges or turns more towards the north, to ALDERSHOT station (North Camp), and thence to FARNBOROUGH, about a mile from the station of the same name on the South Western line.

The line then proceeds through the valley of the Blackwater to

BLACKWATER

A telegraph station. HOTEL – White Hart.

A mile further is SANDHURST Royal Military College, situated to the right of the line, in the centre of a fine park. Peculiar interest attaches to this establishment, from the fact of its being the school where some of our ablest military men have acquired that rudimentary education which they have afterwards turned to such good practical account in the field.

The railway then takes almost a direct line for several miles to

WOKINGHAM

POPULATION, 2,404. Distance from the station, 1 mile. A telegraph station.

HOTEL – Bush. POST HORSES, FLYS etc., at the station and hotels.

FAIR – Whit Tuesday. MONEY ORDER OFFICE at Wokingham.

Wokingham is situated on the River Wey, on the borders of Windsor Forest. The town consist of three streets, with a handsome new Town Hall (modern Gothic) and Market Place in the centre. The Parish Church is picturesque, and undergoing restoration. A new church is also being built by J. Walter, Esq., proprietor of *The Times*. The railways have given considerable impetus to trade here, and house property has become valuable.

From this station the railway passes over a level but highly cultivated country, interspersed with villages and country-seats, until it reaches the terminus at Reading. [Described in Vol. 1 of this series of Bradshaw's Guides.]

South Eastern Main Line continued – Reigate to Tunbridge.

On leaving Reigate, the railway turns off towards the south-east, past the village of Nutfield, a short distance beyond which is Bletchingley, both situated on a range of hills. Bletchingly church is a handsome building containing several fine monuments – and there are the remains of a castle in the neighbourhood.

A little further on, the line passes through Bletchingley Tunnel, and shortly after the train reaches

GODSTONE

Distance from station, 3 miles. A telegraph station. HOTEL – White Hart.

CONVEYANCES – Omnibuses to and from London, through Limpfield, daily.

FAIR – July 22. MONEY ORDER OFFICE at Godstone.

The name of the village adjacent is derived from a corruption of 'good stone', significant of the quarries there worked. There was formerly a mineral spring of some repute a short distance from Godstone. The parks and mansions in the neighbourhood are much admired, and from some of the hills are beautiful views of the surrounding country of Surrey and Kent. Tandridge and Limpsfield are pretty villages, about two miles distant.

Passing over Stafford's Wood Common, the line now traverses a fine and open country, entering the county of Kent at a spot bearing the diminutive cognomen of 'Little Browns'. The intervening miles are rapidly left behind, and we again pause for a few brief minutes at Edenbridge, the first station in the county of Kent.

Kent

This county forms the south-eastern extremity of the island of Great Britain, bounded on the north by the Thames; on the east and south-east by the German Ocean and the Straits of Dover; on the south-west by the English Channel and county of Sussex; on the west by that of Surrey.

From the diversity of its surface, the noble rivers by which it is watered, the richness and variety of its inland scenery, and the most sublime beauties of its sea coast, this

The line between Redhill and Tonbridge is almost dead straight and Godstone station, now unstaffed, is seen in 2006. The name is a corruption of 'good stone', suggestive of the local quarrying industry. *(Arthur Tayler)*

Above: Hever Castle, the birthplace of Anne Boleyn, is close to Edenbridge. *(Laurel Arnison)*

Tonbridge

Although noted for its ancient grammar school and castle, this has long been a major railway centre. First reached by the SER in 1842 (as Tunbridge, later Tunbridge Junction), a branch to Tunbridge Wells opened in September 1845. The present station dates from 1864, in preparation for the arrival of the cut-off line through Sevenoaks, which arrived in 1868. The booking office on the over-bridge was rebuilt in 1958 and the whole station refurbished in 2012. Over 4.2 million people use the station annually. This image shows one of the famous 'Hastings' six-car diesel electric multiple units which plied the London–Hastings road between 1957 and 1986. *(John Atkinson)*

county may be said to rank among the most interesting portions of our island; while the numerous remains of antiquity, the splendid cathedrals, venerable castles, and mouldering monastic edifices, are connected with some of the most remarkable events in English history.

Two chains of hills, called the Upper and Lower, run through the middle of the county from east to west, generally about eight miles asunder; the northern range is part of the extensive ridge which runs through Hampshire and Surrey to Dover, where it terminates in the well known white cliffs. Beyond the southern or lower range is what is called the Weald of Kent, a large tract of rich and fertile land. Kent is essentially and almost solely an agricultural county. The Isle of Thanet is remarkably fertile, but in the Isle of Sheppey only one-fifth of the land is arable; the rest consists of marsh and pasture land, and is used for breeding and fattening sheep and cattle.

The Thames, the Medway, the Stour, the Rother, and the Darent are the principal rivers; while numerous small streams diffuse fertility in every direction.

EDENBRIDGE

A telegraph station.

HOTEL – Albion (at the station).

OMNIBUSES at the station; also at Westerham.

FAIR – May 6th.

MONEY ORDER OFFICE at East Grinstead.

The village of Edenbridge, situated 1 mile from the station, derives its name from the little river Eden, one of the tributary streams of the Medway. There are several chaleybeate springs in the neighbourhood. The church of Edenbridge is a fine ancient edifice, containing several handsome tombs; also a curious monument of the Earl of Wiltshire. A few miles distant is the village of Westerham; and a short distance south of a line is *Hever Castle*, once the residence of the unfortunate Queen Anne Boleyn. The castle was erected in the reign of Edward III by William de Hean. It subsequently fell into the hands of the Cobhams, who disposed of it to Sir Godfrey Boleyn, a rich mercer of London, and great grandfather of Queen Anne Boleyn. It is still an imposing building, and many of the rooms present the same appearance as during the happy visits of Henry VIII. Various shields, with the arms and alliances of the Boleyn family, are displayed on the windows. The castle is still inhabited; it is surrounded by a moat, the entrance embattled and defended by a drawbridge and portcullis. Anne of Cleves died here in 1557.

The village of Chiddingstone, near Hever, is one of the prettiest in the county, and the whole district is remarkable for most beautiful scenery. The neighbourhood here begins to get thronged with objects of attraction sufficient to draw the tourist from his main route.

From Edenbridge station to the next, there are a succession of agreeable prospects, diversified by a few impediments to a good view in the form of an intervening cutting.

Left: Tonbridge is the base for Network Rail's fleet of de-icing trains which keep the lines in Sussex, Surrey and Kent free of snow and ice in winter. *(Pat Searle)*

Left: An Edwardian advertising poster. *(CMcC)*

Tunbridge Wells remains a popular tourist centre, but, following the arrival of the South Eastern Railway's branch from Tonbridge in 1845, it has also developed into a major commuter town, with numerous fast trains to London and over 3.5 million passengers per year.

Below: Rail enthusiasts will be drawn to the Spa Valley Railway, which is based at the engine shed once part of the LBSCR's Tunbridge Wells West station, which arrived from Groombridge in October 1866. Steam and diesel services run to Eridge. The area is part of the High Weald and is renowned for its rock formations, which attract many amateur climbers. The Spa Valley line takes visitors to the High Rocks formation and those at Eridge. *(Simon Jeffs, Laurel Arnison)*

MAGNIFICENT SCENERY. HIGH SUNSHINE RECORD.

ROYAL TUNBRIDGE WELLS

THE KENTISH HEALTH RESORT

FOR OFFICIAL GUIDE
POST FREE 2½d
APPLY TOWN HALL (DEPT III)
ROYAL TUNBRIDGE WELLS

ONE HOUR FROM LONDON.

Every facility for Cricket, Lawn Tennis, Hunting, Golf, Bowls, &c.

STOP

PENSHURST

Distance from station, 2 miles. A telegraph station.

HOTEL – Leicester Arms. POST HORSES, FLYS etc., at the station and hotel.

FAIR – Monday after June 24th. MONEY ORDER OFFICE at Tunbridge.

This is a small but exceedingly pretty village, celebrated for its fine old castle, the property of the Sidney family. This noble structure stands in a magnificent park, and covers a large area with its court, halls and quadrangles. It also contains a valuable collection of paintings, which visitors, by the kindness of the noble owner, are permitted to view.

South Park, the seat and property of the late Lord Hardinge, is two miles distant towards the south, and in a few miles in the opposite direction in the north is the beautiful village of *Seven Oaks*, containing *Knowle Park*, the seat of the Sackvilles – a most picturesque place. The mansion is built in the old English style of architecture, castellated and with square towers. Knowle Mansion and Park form one of the most splendid seats in the kingdom. The collection of paintings is also very fine, and particularly rich in works of the great Italian masters.

Wilderness, the seat of the Marquis of Camden, about two miles beyond Seven Oaks, is a more modern mansion, but most beautifully situated.

A few miles more in the course of which we thrice cross the winding Medway, brings us to

TUNBRIDGE

POPULATION, 5,919. A telegraph station.

MARKET DAY – alternate Tuesdays. FAIR – October 11th.

Situated on the Tun and four branches of the Medway, all crossed by bridges. It is noted for its excellent Grammar School with sixteen exhibitions. The castle, of which a fine noble gateway flanked by round towers still remains, was built by Richard Fitz Gilbert, Earl of Clare and Hertford, who likewise founded a priory here for Augustine Canons, the refectory of which may be seen. Open on Saturdays from 10 till 4, by permission of the proprietor.

This, besides being the branch station for passengers to Tunbridge Wells, has a convenient refreshment-room appended.

Tunbridge Wells and Hastings Branch

Tunbridge Junction to Hastings

The railway commences through a series of deep cuttings, and then proceeds through a tunnel of considerable length. The strata of each side of the line is composed of ironstone and sandstone, diversified with clay, in a manner quite peculiar to the county.

TUNBRIDGE WELLS

POPULATION, about 13,807. A telegraph station.

HOTELS – The Calverley; Kentish Royal; Royal Sussex.

OMNIBUSES to and from the station, also to Paddock Wood.

POST HORSES, FLYS, etc., at the station and hotels. MARKET DAYS – Daily.

This town is, with the exception of Bath, the most ancient of the inland watering places. Nature has eminently favoured it by the salubrity of its air, the potency of its mineral springs, and the adjacent appendages of romantic and agreeable scenery. Dudley Lord North, a young nobleman of the Court of James I, while on a visit to Eridge House, happened to taste the waters, and these renovating a constitution impaired by too much indulgence, caused him to bring the place into fashionable repute. From that time visitors gradually increased, streets were laid out, lodging-houses built, and now, through the caprice of fashion has somewhat depreciated the fame of our own spas, Tunbridge Wells may still boast a large share of patronage in the season, which extends from May till November. The town is built upon a sandy soil, and is divided into five districts, called respectively, Mount Ephraim, Mount Pleasant, Mount Sion, the Wells and the Sew, at the latter of which is a new church (St John's) has been built. The town has been much modernised of late years, the Parade alone evincing any symptoms of antiquity. The houses are chiefly detached villas, with lawns in front, and large gardens in the rear. Those that are situated on the mounts have extensive views, that combine hill and dale, forests and fields, commons, meadows, and corn lands, with a large tract of hop-grounds. The drinking springs rise at the end of the Parade, close to the Post Office, which has a row of trees on one side, and a colonnade with shops on the other. The water is a strong chalybeate, and possesses great tonic power, but ought not to be taken without medical advice. A band plays three times a day on the Parade in the season, from July until November. The ex-queen of the French visits the town annually, but the usual gaieties have long since declined. The climate is congenial, and the air upon the downs has a fine bracing and exhilarating property. There is almost perfect immunity from fog, and being sheltered from the north-east winds by the north downs, the temperature throughout the year is pleasant and equable. The inns and boarding-houses are generally of a superior description. There are billiard rooms on the Parade and at the Castle Hotel, and photographs at Woods, Mount Ephraim. The manufacture of wooden toys and articles of domestic use, long celebrated as 'Tunbridge Ware', is still carried on here to a considerable extent, and was formerly the principal produce of the place. Tunbridge Common is a most delightful resort in the summer; the old racecourse still exists, but is not used; a new cricket grounds has been made where many matches are held. The old chapel has a sun dial with the following inscription: 'You may waste but cannot stop me.'

Excursions may be made to the Eridge Rocks, about a mile and a half south-west of the town; they are of considerable height, surrounded with wood, and much admired by visitors; Wednesday and Thursday. *Eridge Park* the property of Lord Abergavenny, is one of the most delightful walks in the vicinity. Start from the Parade, and proceed along the Frant road, branching off through the woods to the

54

right; Penshurst, five miles distant, Penshurst Place, a quadrangular building of the Elizabethan style of architecture, Monday and Saturday; Crowborough Common, at the Beacon, seven miles from the Wells, stands on an elevation of 800 feet above the level of the sea; Eridge Castle, two miles distant; Hever, seven miles distant; *Southborough*, two and a half miles, at which there is a noble cricket ground, in great request among the clubs in the neighbourhood, there is also a smaller one on Southborough Common; *Summerhill*, two miles, a fine Elizabethan building, once the residence of the Earl of Leicester and General Lambert; *Oxenheath*, four miles; and Bayham Abbey, the seat of the Marquis of Camden, six miles distant, the ruins being exceedingly picturesque. The modern mansion is in the Gothic style. Tuesday and Friday, the High Rocks, Brambletye Ruins, and Toad Rock. There are other fine seats and handsome villas in the vicinity, and the environs of Tunbridge abound in beautiful walks and drives.

From Tunbridge Wells the railway proceeds southward and enters the county of Sussex, passing through a short tunnel at starting, and then proceeds through a deep cutting.

FRANT

Distance from the station, 1 mile. A telegraph station.

HOTELS – Spread Eagle and Abergavenny Arms.

MONEY ORDER OFFICE at Tunbridge Wells.

A short distance from this station is *Eridge Castle*, the demesne of the Earl of Abergavenny, situated in a noble park, well stocked with deer. There are several handsome villas in the neighbourhood, the scenery of which is exceedingly varied, and some of the views of the country around are both extensive and beautiful.

Between Frant and Robertsbridge the scenery becomes less picturesque, though the country is highly cultivated, and the hop-grounds are particularly fine. Near the Wadhurst station there is rather a long tunnel, and the church of Wadhurst is worthy of a visit.

WADHURST

Distance from station, 1 mile. A telegraph station.

MARKET DAY – Saturday. FAIRS – April 29th and November 1st.

MONEY ORDER OFFICE at Wadhurst.

TICEHURST ROAD

Distance from station, 1 mile. A telegraph station.

MARKET DAYS – Sat. FAIRS – May 4 and Oct 7.

MONEY ORDER OFFICE at Ticehurst.

Ticehurst is rather a large town, situated on high ground, about three miles and a half to the east of the station, in the midst of a splendid agricultural country.

Battle

1066 is a date seared into the memory of every British schoolchild as this was the date when the English army, led by King Harold, was defeated by William the Conqueror's Norman army at a location in Sussex now known as Battle. William erected an abbey to commemorate his victory, around which the town of Battle grew. *(Laurel Arnison)*

The abbey remains a tourist magnet, patronage increasing when the SER extended its line from Tunbridge Wells to the town in 1852 and provided it with a splendid station. Indeed, many of the stations on this line are very pleasing.

Above and right: The station at Frant. *(Simon Jeffs, Ashley Saunders)*

56

ETCHINGHAM

Distance from station, 1 mile. A telegraph station.
MONEY ORDER OFFICE at Wadhurst.

The church at Etchingham is a fine old edifice, reputed to be one of the best specimens of Norman architecture in the country.

The stations at Frant, Etchingham and Battle are built in the Gothic character; those at Wadhurst, Ticehurst Road and Robertsbridge are in the Italian style, of red and white brick and Caen stone.

ROBERTSBRIDGE

Distance from station, ¼ mile. A telegraph station. HOTEL – Old George.
MARKET DAY – Thursday. MONEY ORDER OFFICE at Robertsbridge.

The village is situated on the banks of the river Rother and only remarkable for the houses being constructed of red brick, which gives the place a peculiar appearance.

BATTLE

Distance from station, 1 mile. A telegraph station. HOTEL – George.
OMNIBUSES to and from the station. MARKET DAY – The second Monday in each month. FAIRS – Whit Monday and November 22nd.

This town was formerly called Epiton, and received its present name from being the spot on which the Saxons, under Harold, were defeated by William the Duke of Normandy, in 1066. After the contest the Conqueror founded a magnificent abbey to commemorate his victory, and the high altar in the church is said to have stood on the very spot where the body of the heroic Saxon prince was found. The noble gateway of the abbey has a fine effect when seen from the town. In the abbey was formerly preserved the celebrated Battle Abbey Roll, which formed a list of those families which came over from Normandy with the Duke.

The mingled scene of hill and dale, wood and village, presents one of those fair spots in nature which refresh the traveller who, hurrying through tunnel and cutting, to annihilate time and space, too often disregards the beauty of the country through which he passes.

Four miles further is ST LEONARDS STATION

HASTINGS

POPULATION, 22,910. A telegraph station.
HOTELS – The Marine, on the Parade; Albion; Castle.
OMNIBUSES to and from the station to meet every train.
POST HORSES, FLYS, etc., at the hotels and station, to meet every train.
MARKET DAYS – Saturdays (corn); daily (poultry).
FAIRS – Whit Tuesday, July 26 and 29, and November 27.

The recognised salubrity and mildness of the air, together with the openness of the

Etchingham is on the road to Burwash, where the home of Rudyard Kipling, Batemans (National Trust), can be visited. Nice though the stations are, the line was built very cheaply with narrow tunnels and a poorly-constructed permanent way. For years, narrow-bodied trains had to be provided to fit through the tunnels, the lines through them being singled when the Tonbridge–St Leonards line was electrified in 1986. At the time of writing (March 2014), the line is closed between Robertsbridge and Battle following extensive landslips after heavy rain. *(Simon Jeffs)*

Hastings, with its castle, founded by William the Conquerer in 1070, caves, two funicular railways, old town and traditional seaside entertainments. It still has a pier, on which restoration has just commenced following the tragic fire which nearly destroyed it on 5 October 2010. *(Simon Jeffs)*

coast and the smoothness of the beach, have long made Hastings a favourite and a recommended resort. The shore is not abrupt, and the water almost always limpid, and of that beautiful sea-green hue so inviting to bathers. The constant surging of the waves, first breaking against the reefs, and next dashing over the sloping shingle, is not unwelcome music at midnight to the ears of all who *sleep* in the vicinity of the shore. Dr James Clark states, that in winter Hastings is most desirable as a place of residence during January and February.

> During the spring also it has the advantage of being more effectively sheltered from north and north-east winds than any other place frequented by invalids on the coast of Sussex. It is also comparatively little subject to fogs in the spring, and the fall of rain may be said at that time to be less than on other portions of the coast. As might be expected from the low and sheltered situation of Hastings, it will be found a favourable residence generally to invalids suffering under diseases of the chest. Delicate persons, who desire to avoid exposure to the north-east winds, may pass the cold season here with advantage. Owing to the close manner in which this place is hemmed in on the sea by steep and high cliffs, it has an atmosphere more completely marine than almost any other part of the coast, with the exception, of course, of St Leonards, which possesses the same dry and absorbent soil.

The breadth and extent of its esplanade also, and the protection afforded by the colonnades for walking exercise, are circumstances of considerable importance to the invalid, and render a conjoined residence at Hastings and St Leonards a very efficient substitute for a trip to Madeira.

The Castle of Hastings, for a time the favourite residence of the Conqueror, has remained a mass of magnificent ruins; its towers, bastions, and ancient walls forming an object truly picturesque, as seen from any point of view, but looking even grand in their sombre desolation, as meeting the eye of the pedestrian when ascending the eminence leading to Fairlight Downs.

A few years back the visitors to the castle were shown *two* coffins, a small one and a larger one, which they were assured contained the ashes of a mother and infant. These have been lately removed, and the space of ground enclosed by walls which used to shelter such vestiges of a more barbarous age is now employed by a market gardener to administer to the culinary wants of the townsfolk of Hastings and St Leonards.

The approach to Hastings Castle is from the further extremity of Wellington Square, and, with the perpendicular cliff that fronts the sea for its base, the outer walls appear originally to have had the form of a triangle with rounded angles. For some time past the interior has been laid out as a flower garden and shrubbery, and the person who has charge of the lodge accommodates, for a small fee, visitors with seats and refreshments. The view, though not equal to that from Fairlight Downs, is varied and extensive, and commands towards the south an ample marine expanse, while Beachy Head, Eastbourne and Bexhill may be seen towards the west.

While in the neighbourhood, it should not be forgotten that a delightful excursion

Until the development of tourism, fishing was Hastings' major industry. The fishing fleet, based at the Stade, remains Europe's largest beach-launched fishing fleet and has been based on the same beach for at least 400, possibly 600, years. The Stade/Rock-a-Noor area also houses a fishing museum, backed by the traditional black net houses, smugglers' museum, aquarium and the Jerwood Gallery of modern art. *(Simon Jeffs)*

Left: The SER line from Battle finally arrived in the Hastings in 1852. A new, modern structure has recently been provided, with a very convenient bus interchange. *(Simon Jeffs)*

may be made to Battle Abbey, not more than six miles distant. The grounds are now in possession of the Webster family, who have liberally thrown them open to public inspection every Friday at 1.30 p.m. It is here that the 'Battel Roll', a sort of primitive 'Court Guide', is carefully preserved, and furnishes a list valuable to the antiquary and historian of those families who came over with William the Conqueror.

A glance into the booksellers' windows, where engraved vignettes of some neighbouring attraction allure the eye in every direction, will at once reveal to the visitor the tempting beauty of the environs. A week may be delightfully spent in exploring the fairy-like nooks about Fairlight alone. Situated in a sweet umbrageous spot, down which, by narrow winding steps, hewn out of the solid rock, one can only descend at a time, is the weeping rock. The view of the constantly dripping well, as the spectator looks up to the jutting rock from the beautiful cottage of Covehurst below, is well calculated to inspire the mind with that feeling under which credence would be given to any legend that accounted for this freak of nature, by ascribing it to the influence of supernatural agency. The stone weeps, as it were, from myriads of pores, and although the water falls in continuous drops, no trace is left of it in the reservoir; passing through the rock, its appearance is as mysterious as its disappearance is magical. It is explained by the soil beneath being loose and sandy, over a heavy beach stone foundation, and, acting as a subterraneous drain, the water is conducted beneath the surface, appearing as a truculent stream about a hundred yards from the rock, and then again disappearing down a declivity. The beautiful appearance the rock presents in winter, when the drip is frozen and the icicles hang from the sloping crags in clusters of crystals, will not be easily forgotten by those who have had the good fortune to witness, at this period, such a mimic stalactite cavern.

Then in the vicinity of the well are the fish-ponds with romantic walks around it, and a comfortable farmhouse adjacent, where refreshments can be had at a small cost, and where the ale is – but we forebear our eloquence. The picturesque waterfall of Old Roar should not be overlooked, nor the Lover's Seat, so charmingly enthroned amid shrubs and evergreens, nor the favoured localities, which are enough to make a Pennsylvanian lawyer turn poetical. Let the pedestrian, however, make his way to the signal house belonging to the coast-guard station at that point, and he will have a panoramic view around him which it would be worth his while walking from Cornhill to Grand Cairo only to behold and then walk back again.

The whole forms a complete circle; the sweep of inland scenery extending to the hills in the neighbourhood of London, and the sea view reaching from Beachy Head to Dover Cliffs, between seventy and eighty miles apart, and stretching out to the heights of Boulogne. The entire area of the prospect, both by land and water, cannot be less than three hundred miles. Among many minor objects visible may be enumerated ten towns, sixty-six churches, seventy Martello towers, five ancient castles, three bays, and forty windmills. The best time for seeing it is the afternoon, when the setting sun lights up the old town of Hastings in the foreground, and brings into strong shadow the opposite coast of France. Upon favourable atmospheric influences it is, indeed, a view never to be forgotten.

Paddock Wood/Yalding/Wateringbury
Above: The branch to Maidstone (now Maidstone West) was opened from Paddock Wood in September 1844, and was joined to Strood by 1856, the new through station at Maidstone not being completed until 1858. The line follows the River Medway throughout, traversing rich farming country south of Maidstone which, in Bradshaw's day, was predominantly given over to the cultivation of the 'Kentish Vine' – Hops. *(Don Benn)*

The stations were very mean affairs when the line opened, but new, stone-built structures replaced them when the line was doubled by 1846. Those at Yalding and Wateringbury are shown, *left*. Despite its beauty, the line is poorly-used south of Maidstone, its major users being weekend walkers and (formally) anglers. *(Ashley Saunders)*

South Eastern Main Line continued.

Tunbridge to Paddock Wood.
Leaving Tunbridge, the line passes through the beautiful park of *Summerhill*, property of Baron de Goldschmidt, and thence, on past the villages of Tudely and Capel to the

PADDOCK WOOD JUNCTION.
A telegraph station. MONEY ORDER OFFICE at Tunbridge.

Maidstone Branch.

Paddock Wood to Maidstone.

The branch to Maidstone from Paddock Wood follows the course of the Medway throughout, and enables the traveller to snatch some rapid glimpses of a woody country, presenting the true characteristics of a Kentish landscape. On each side of us we find the land studded with substantial homesteads and wealthy looking farms, rising in the midst of corn fields or orchards, or surrounded by the British vineyards, the Kentish hop-grounds.

YALDING
Distance from station, 1½ miles. A telegraph station.
FAIR – October 15th. MONEY ORDER OFFICE at Maidstone.

The village of Yalding is not remarkable for anything of interest to the traveller. A short distance from it are Yalding Downs and Barnes Hill; and to the left of the station there are several country seats and mansions, in most beautiful parks.

WATERINGBURY
Distance from station, ½ mile. A telegraph station. HOTEL – Duke's Head
MONEY ORDER OFFICE at Maidstone.

This is a large and handsome village, retaining its rural character, combined with an unusual degree of charming neatness and taste. The cottage gardens are sweetly pretty. The church is rather handsome, and contains several tombs of the Style family. Wateringbury Place in the vicinity is a fine mansion, situated in very beautiful grounds.

A mile beyond, above the line, is the neat village of Teston, the scenery around which, with the bridge across the Medway, is quite picturesque. *Barham Court*, the mansion and Park of the Earl of Gainsborough, is in the vicinity. There are several unusually pretty villages and villas on the right side of the river and railway. East and West Farleigh, on the banks of the Medway, though consisting only of scattered houses, are exceedingly

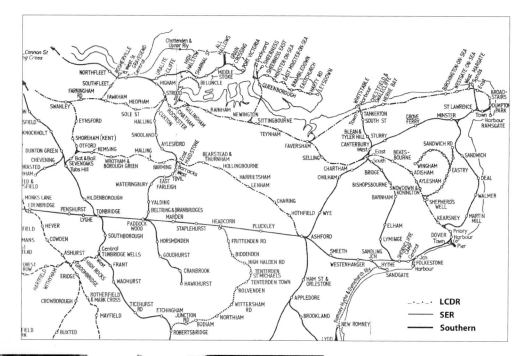

Above: Kent rail map, 1976.

Maidstone, the county town, has a population of over 113,000. Paper mills, stone quarrying, brewing and the cloth industry have all flourished here. Aylesford (to the north-west) has the largest paper recycling factory in Europe, making newsprint, and the area is a base for the paper and packaging industry. The railway arrived in 1844, but, due to a desire to reach Dover by the easiest route, was bypassed by the SER main line. *(Peter de Russett)*

A secondary route from Swanley Junction to Maidstone East provided the town with a second route to London in 1871 but both are relatively slow. The situation improved in May 2011, when three high speed train services a day in each direction were provided to London St Pancras, taking around fifty minutes. One of these services is pictured at Snodland. *(Colin Scott-Morton)*

pleasing. The church in the latter place is a very ancient one covered with ivy, and, with the hop-grounds and orchards, has quite a sylvan appearance.

EAST FARLEIGH

Is close to the bridge over the Medway.

A telegraph station. MONEY ORDER OFFICE at Maidstone.

Two miles beyond this the train enters the present terminus of this line at Maidstone. It is a very neat and commodious structure, within a few minutes' walk of the High-street.

MAIDSTONE.

Population, 23,058. Distance from station ¼ mile. A telegraph station.

HOTELS – The Mitre; The Royal Star and Bell.

OMNIBUSES to and from station, also to London direct, and to Faversham via Debtling, Stocksbury Valleys, Key Street, Sittingbourne, Milton, Rochester, Chatham, Strood, and Canterbury.

POST HORSES, FLYS, etc., at the hotels.

MARKET DAYS – Thursdays and Saturdays. FAIRS – 2nd Tuesday in every month (cattle), Feb 13th, May 12th, June 20th, Oct. 17th (Hops).

MONEY ORDER OFFICE at Maidstone.

BANKERS – The London and County Joint Stock Bank. Mercer, Randall, and Co.

Maidstone is a parliamentary borough, and the capital of Kent, on the Medway, in a tract of land of great fertility, among orchards, hop grounds and woodlands. The distance from London has been recently reduced 13 miles by the opening of the North Kent line from Strood. It is not only a shorter route, but commands a splendid view of the valley of the Medway and the adjacent hills.

The town is on the slopes of the hills, so that, rising from the banks of the river, at the north entrances are the cavalry barracks (of wood!), and the county jail, the latter being a most complete and extensive pile, nearly two-thirds of a mile round its quadrangular wall, and covering 14 acres. It includes the assize courts, and was built in 1829, of the ragstone which is so abundant in the neighbourhood. The county asylum occupies a site of 37 acres. In High-street stands the old brick Town Hall, over the corn market, the butter market being in an adjoining street.

Round the church are grouped some interesting remains. The church itself is an embattled straggling building of great length, nearly 230 ft; and was made collegiate by Archbishop Courtenay, who is buried here in the middle of the chancel. His arms are over the old stalls and stone seats on the south side. It was here that the royalists were surrounded by Fairfax when he took the town, after a hard fight, in 1648.

The Primates had a palace here from King John's time, of which a part, still inhabited, hangs over the river on one side of the churchyard. Another old looking house is styled the castle; behind, are ruins of Courtenay's College, of which Grocyn, the Greek scholar,

Staplehurst

This station, on the almost dead-straight 'racing stretch' between Tonbridge and Ashford, would be of little note were it not for the train crash that occurred here on 9 June 1865. The SER Folkestone–London boat train derailed while crossing a viaduct, where a length of track had been removed during engineering works, killing ten passengers and injuring forty. Charles Dickens was travelling with Ellen Ternan and her mother on the train. The experience affected him greatly and he emained nervous when travelling by train, using alternative means when available. Dickens died five years to the day after the accident, his son stating that he had never fully recovered.

Headcorn is the railhead for two local castles. Leeds Castle, *above*, dates from 1119 and was the residence of Henry VIII's first wife, Catherine of Aragon. The castle was remodelled in 1823 and is open to the public. In contrast, Sissinghurst Castle (strictly, a fortified manor house) only retains its Elizabethan tower but is renowned for its gardens, created in the 1930s by Vita Sackville-West and her husband Harold Nicolson. These are considered one of the finest in England and the site is now owned by the National Trust. *(Adusha)*

and friend of Erasmus, was for a while master; after teaching at Oxford he was buried here. Here also are fragments of a priory, and the Grammar School. There is a great air of quiet antiquity about this part of Maidstone. In West-Borough (over the bridge) is the ancient chapel of a hospital founded in the 13th century by Archbishop Boniface, while another chapel (now a school) was occupied by the Walloons, or Dutch Protestants, expelled by the Spanish butcher Alva, in Elizabeth's time. The flax spun here for thread is still called Dutch work, in remembrance of the persecuted emigrants. William Hazlitt was a native of Maidstone, born 1778.

In the ragstone quarried here Dr Mantell found his fossil *iguanodon*, which he thinks must have been nearly 70 ft long. A restoration of this river-monster is at the Crystal Palace.

Besides hops, cherries, filberts, etc., paper is a staple production, especially at the Turkey and Pole mills, on the Len; and the Toril mills, near the old pest house up the Medway. Coppices for hop-poles, props, etc., are dispersed about. The hop was first cultivated in Kent in the time of Henry VI, about the middle of the 15th century.

The walk along the Rochester road to Blue Bell Down (4 miles) affords a charming panorama of orchards, copses and hills; and the views from the Down itself amply repay the long ascent to it.

South Eastern Main Line continued – Paddock Wood to Ashford

From Paddock the main line proceeds rapidly in the direction of the coast, and although the country presents very charming alternations of waste and woodland scenery, yet it does not offer objects of sufficient interest to describe in detail. Views of the hop fields are shut in by excavations which, like the change of slides in dissolving views, transform the landscape every moment.

MARDEN

Distance from station, ¼ mile. A telegraph station.
FAIR – October 11. MONEY ORDER OFFICE at Staplehurst.

The only object of notice is Marden church. *Boughton Place* in the neighbourhood is a very fine estate, from some points of which may be obtained several extensive views over the Weald of Kent.

Two miles more and the train reaches the station at

STAPLEHURST

A telegraph station. HOTELS – South Eastern, King's Head.
FAIRS – Monday after July 20th, Wednesday after September 20th.
MONEY ORDER OFFICE.

The village of the same name is quite near the station; its fine old church and quaint antique houses are much admired.

The village of Cranbrook, in the heart of the Weald of Kent is remarkable for its

Ashford

International services through the Channel Tunnel started on 8 January 1996, following the rebuilding and renaming of the station as Ashford International. Before the completion of High Speed 1 in November 2007, twelve Eurostar trains to Paris and Brussels called but, following the opening of Ebbsfleet station, this has been controversially reduced to five daily. A high-speed domestic service operated by Southeastern to London St Pancras began on 29 June 2009, with trains taking only thirty-eight minutes to London St Pancras International. As a result of this, Ashford has expanded massively and is now a major commuting centre with 3.3 million domestic passenger movements annually. *(Simon Jeffs)*

Wye College was founded in 1447 by John Kempe, the Archbishop of York, as a college for the training of priests, but in 1894, the school moved to new premises, and the South Eastern Agricultural College was established in the buildings. Famous for its development of many varieties of hops, it was officially closed by its then owner, Imperial College London, in September 2009 and is now a free school. The station lies in the valley of the River Stour on the line between Ashford and Margate via Canterbury (now Canterbury West), opened in 1846. *(Bryan Rayner)*

handsome church, considered one of the most interesting edifices in the county. The remains of Sissinghurst Castle, four miles, are also well worth a visit.

HEADCORN

Distance from station, ½ mile. A telegraph station.
HOTELS – The George, King's Arms. MARKET – Wednesday. FAIR – June 12th.
MONEY ORDER OFFICE at Staplehurst.

This village possesses no feature of particular or general interest, beyond the splendid old oak tree in the churchyard. The churches of Chart Sutton, Sutton Valance, and Sutton Castle, are worth visiting.

From Headcorn the railway passes the villages of Smarden and Bedenham on the right side, and then reaches

PLUCKLEY

Distance from station, 1¼ miles. A telegraph station. FAIRS – Whit Mondays
(Toys and Pedlery), Feast of St Nicholas (cattle). MONEY ORDER OFFICE, Ashford.

In the neighbourhood of Pluckley there are several villages and country seats. *Bethersden* the seat of the Lovelaces, a family now extinct, two and a half miles. Great Chart, once a large market town, and many others. Leeds Castle, however, in general absorbs the attention of the traveller. Of Norman architecture, situated in a beautiful park, and being still in good preservation, it is one of the most imposing and interesting castles in the county of Kent.

ASHFORD

POPULATION, 5,522. Distance from station, ½ miles. A telegraph station.
HOTELS – The Victoria, near the railway station; Saracen's Head; Royal Oak.
MARKET DAYS – Every Tuesday (corn), 1st, 3rd and 5th Tuesday in every
month (cattle). FAIRS – May 17th, Sept 12th, and Oct 24th for horses, cattle
and pedlery. MONEY ORDER OFFICE at Ashford.
BANKERS – London and County Joint Stock Bank. Jemmet and Co.

This was a quiet agricultural town in East Kent till the South Eastern Railway Company made it the chief station for their works, since which the population has greatly increased. It is on the Stour, at the junction of the branches to Canterbury, Margate and Hastings, with the main line to Dover, from which it is 21 miles. Among the buildings erected by the company are a carriage house 645 ft long; a repairing shop, 395 ft by 45; an engine room 210 ft by 63; beside factories for wheels, boilers, etc. Such is the wear and tear a wheel undergoes that it requires to be fresh turned after every 2,000 miles of travelling. A church has also been built for their workmen, by the company. The parish church is a large and handsome edifice, in the Gothic style, containing several brass and stone monuments of the families of the neighbourhood – as the Smythes of Westenhanger, the Fogges of Repton, etc.

Three miles N.E. is *Eastwell Park*, the seat of the Earl of Winchelsea, standing on a ridge which commands a view of the Thames on one side and the British Channel on the other. There is an extensive lake in the park, with a pretty model ship of war floating on it, fully rigged. The church contains many tombs of the Finches and Moyles; but the most remarkable monument if that to Richard Plantagenet, the last descendant of that royal house, who died here in obscurity as a bricklayer to the Moyles, 22nd Dec, 1550. His name is inserted in the register book under that date. The story concerning him is that he never knew who his father was till the Battle of Bosworth Field, when he was taken into Leicestershire, and carried to Richard III's tent. The king embraced him and told him he was his son.

> But child (says he), to-morrow I must fight for my crown, and if I lose that I will lose my life too. If I should be so unfortunate, shift as well as you can, and take care to let nobody know that I am your father, for no mercy will be shown anyone so near to me.

When the battle was lost he sold his horse and his fine clothes, and, to hide all suspicion of his descent, put himself apprentice to a bricklayer. In this situation he was discovered reading a Latin book by his employer Sir T. Moyle, to whom he told his secret as it has come down to us. Not long ago there was a brick house in the park built by Richard. His singular fate is the subject of a very charming book called the *Last of the Plantagenets*.

Within two or three miles of Ashford are the following seats: *Merstham Hatch*, Sir Norton Knatchbull, Bart.; *Hothfield*, Sir R. Tufton, Bart., for ages the seat of the Thanet (or Tufton family), and near Ripley, whose Sheriff Iden seized and killed Jack Cade, who was hiding here. *Surrenden*, an ancient family seat of the Derings, descended from the Sir Edward whose sufferings in the civil war are eloquently described by Southey in the *Book of the Churches. Godington*, N. Toke, Esq., was the seat of Sheriff Toke, a hearty, vigorous man, who died 1680, when ninety-three years old, having walked to London a little before to court his sixth wife. He and his sour predecessors at Godington counted 430 years among them.

All this east end of the Weald of Kent is thick with woodlands, like the rest of that fertile tract, but the roads are damp and heavy.

Ashford and Canterbury Branch

Ashford To Canterbury, Ramsgate Etc.

Here the line branches off to Canterbury, Whitstable, Sandwich, Deal, Ramsgate and Margate, and, from the accommodation it affords to the towns through which it passes, and the exquisite beauty of the scenery along its route, will not suffer in comparison with any line of similar length in the kingdom. It follows throughout the meanderings of the river Stour, and traversing the most fertile districts in the country, has one uninterrupted panorama of luxuriant fertility during its whole length.

On leaving Ashford, the little villages of Brook and Wye are passed in succession to the right, imbedded in a valley sheltered by rising hills, and thickly studded with lofty and umbrageous patches of woodland.

WYE

Distance from station, ½ mile. A telegraph station.
OMNIBUSES to and from Faversham, daily. FAIRS – May 29 and October 11.
MONEY ORDER OFFICE at Wye.

The town of Wye is close to the river Stour, and consists of two main streets. It has a handsome church, and was once a royal manor, granted by William the Conqueror to the Abbey of Battle. Here was a monastic college, the remains of which are still to be seen. Emerging from a tolerably deep cutting, we next trace to the left a most charming and picturesque village, and shortly reach

CHILHAM

Distance from station, ¾ mile. A telegraph station.
OMNIBUSES to and from the station; also to Godmersham and Canterbury.
FAIR – November 8th. MONEY ORDER OFFICE at Canterbury.

Chilham House or Manor is a noble building, situated in beautiful grounds, which command extensive views over the entire Vale of Ashford and the Stour.

Thence the windings of the Stour, spanned ever and anon by some rustic bridge of wood or stone, enhances the romantic beauty of the landscape, and we seem to be for many miles treading the sylvan labyrinth of a miniature Rhine-land. Shortly afterwards,

The Canterbury & Whitstable Railway was a purely local affair. Services to London awaited the arrival of SER Ashford–Margate line in 1846, whose station is now Canterbury West. *('GB')*

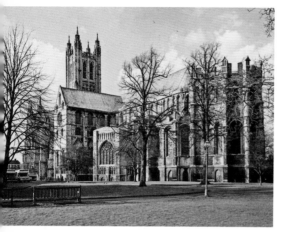

Canterbury

Once a Roman city, *Durovernum Cantiacorum*, Canterbury gained the name *Cantwareburh* ('Kent people's stronghold') from the succeeding Jutes. After the Kingdom of Kent's conversion to christianity in 597, St Augustine founded an episcopal see with cathedral in the city and became the first Archbishop of Canterbury. Thomas Becket's murder in 1170 led to it becoming a place of pilgrimage, providing the theme for Geoffrey Chaucer's *The Canterbury Tales*. One of the most famous religious structures in the world, rebuilt from 1070 many other historical structures remain, including a Roman city wall, the ruins of St Augustine's Abbey, a Norman castle, medieval city gates and perhaps the oldest school in England, The King's School.

Invicta was the fifth locomotive built by Robert Stephenson's foundry in Newcastle, and immediately followed the more famous *Rocket*. It is shown in this postcard, *c.* 1903, being moved to the Dane John Garden, opposite Canterbury station, where it went on display after a long period working on the Canterbury & Whitstable Railway. The traction engine bearing a plate for Canterbury Corporation was built by the Kent company Aveling & Porter. *(CMcC)*

the towers of Canterbury Cathedral rise into sight, followed by the lofty buildings of the city itself, and while watching the course of the railway to Whitstable, which branches off to the north, the accustomed warning sound of the whistle rings in our ears, and we glide beneath the commodious structure of the station at

CANTERBURY

In the western suburb. A telegraph station. POPULATION, 21,324.

HOTELS – Royal Fountain; Rose; Fleur-de-lis.

OMNIBUSES to the station; also to Barham, Dover, Ellam, Elmstead, Faversham, Goodnestone, Wye, Sittingbourne and Eastry.

MARKET DAYS – Wednesdays and Saturdays. FAIRS – May 4th and October 11th.

MONEY ORDER OFFICE. BANKERS – London and County Bank. Hammond & Co.

The appearance of Canterbury, from whatever part approached, is exquisitely beautiful, and as we enter, symbols of antiquity stare us in the face everywhere; narrow passages, crazy tenements, with over-hanging windows, peaked gables, and wooden balustrades, jut out on every side. Here and there some formless sculpture of a fractured cherub or grotesque image, peer out from a creaking doorway. Crypts and vaults seem natural to every house, and yet withal, an air of liveliness pervades the town, that renders the contrast truly pleasing and striking. The city lies in a fertile vale, sheltered by gently rising hills, from which streams of excellent water are derived.

When Becket was murdered here, 1170, in the great contest between the civil and ecclesiastical powers, Canterbury became the centre of pilgrimages from all quarters of Christendom to his shrine. Many old timbered houses, and small ancient rough-cast churches are seen here; but the noble *Cathedral* is the first object of notice as it rises above the town.

It is a double cross 574 feet long inside, with an east transept of 159 feet, and a west one of 128 feet. The oldest part is the half Norman choir, begun 1174; the nave and west transept finished 1420; the great tower is 235 feet high; the west tower is 130 feet. The west front of the great window is of Richard II's time. On one side is a beautiful porch, built as late as 1517. The north-west transept, called the Martyrdom, because Becket was killed there, has a beautifully stained window; the opposite one contains the monuments of Cardinal Langton and the Duke of Clarence. A decorated screen leads into the choir, with the monuments of Archbishops Kemp, Stratford, Sudbury, etc.; those of Chicheley, Bourchier, and other primates, with Henry IV and Queen Joan, the Black Prince and Archbishop of Canterbury, etc., are near Trinity Chapel, in the north-east transept. Here stood Becket's shrine, or the gold chest containing his bones, which Erasmus saw; it shone and sparkled, he says, 'with rare and precious jewels, the chief of them gifts of kings'. During the jubilee of 1420, in an ignorant and superstitious age, as many as 100,000 worshippers crowded to the shrine, expecting to obtain heaven *per Tomæ sanguinem*, 'by the blood of St Thomas', whose chief merit was rebellion to his sovereign. The hollows worn by the knees of devotees may be observed in the pavement. In one year their offerings amounted to £954 6s 3d, while at the Virgin Mary altar in the crypt there were only £4 1s 8d, and at the high (or Christ's) altar, *nothing*. The bones were burnt at the reformation. At the east end of the cathedral is Becket's crown, a chapel so called, where are monuments of Cardinal Chatillon, etc., and the ancient chair of the primates. Below is a very curious Norman crypt, where the Walloons and the Protestant refugees used to meet for worship.

Near this splendid pile are the cloisters, with 811 coats of arms placed round; the later English chapter house, in which Henry II did penance in sackcloth, two years after Becket's death; the Archbishop's deserted palace; baptistry and treasury; the beautiful gate of the Abbey, under which Augustine was buried; and the new missionary college, founded by H. Hope Esq., built in the Gothic style, 1849. St George, St Paul, Holy Cross and St Martin's churches are among the most ancient – especially the last, which stands outside the town, on the site of the first one built by Augustine, having an ivy-covered tower, and the font in which Etheldred was baptised. It has been restored lately with great care. Riding Gate is in Watling Street, on the old road from London, which Chaucer's pilgrims travelled from the Tabard in Southwark, and put up at Chaucer's Inn, in Mercery Lane here, of which few traces are left. Close to this gate is the Donjon or Dane John Terrace, a pleasant spot, laid out as a public walk, and which presents a most gay and lively scene when the elite of the neighbourhood assemble here, once weekly, to enjoy their favourite opera airs, skilfully played by the band of the regiment that may be quartered at the barracks. Westgate is near this; and some other portions of the city walls remain.

Canterbury has a Guildhall, sessions house, cavalry and other barracks, with several schools and hospitals. St Nicholas's hospital, at Harbledown, was founded by Archbishop Lanfranc in the 11th century. That part of the neighbourhood near the Dover road, is dotted all over with fine seats.

Above left and right: The SER also opened offices in the town in the historic street of Mercery Lane. The LCDR also opened a station on its line between Victoria, Faversham and Dover, later becoming Canterbury East, in July 1860. *('GB')*

Canterbury and Whitstable Branch

Canterbury to Whitstable

WHITSTABLE

Distance from station, ¼ mile. A telegraph station. HOTELS – Two Brewers; Bear and Key. OMNIBUSES to and from the station; also to Faversham.
FAIR – Thursday before Whit-Sunday. MONEY ORDER OFFICE at Whitstable

WHITSTABLE is the harbour of Canterbury, and is celebrated for its oyster fishery, the produce of which, under the name of natives, is highly esteemed in the London and other markets. The town, though rather mean in appearance, and irregularly built, has a bustling and thriving appearance, from its fishing and coal trade.

Ashford, Canterbury and Ramsgate Branch continued.

Canterbury to Deal, Ramsgate and Margate

Quitting the Canterbury station, the line proceeds through a similar fertile tract to that which accompanied its progress thither. Cattle grazing knee-deep in luxuriant pastures, farmhouses, cottages and orchards on one side, and sunny fields, rich in corn and clover, sloping down on the other; these are the chief characteristics of the route for the next eleven miles.

Whitstable
Famous for its Oysters! The railway from Canterbury reached in 1830, but the LCDR main line did not arrive until August 1860, on its way to Herne Bay and Ramsgate. *(James Aston)*

Minster and Richborough

At the railway junction of Minster, one may either head east towards Ramsgate and Margate, or south through Sandwich and Deal towards Dover. Images of this location seem to be very rare, shown left is a newly-constructed 4 Cep electric multiple unit on a training run at Minster, 1 March 1961. This was a Phase II unit, built for the second phase of the Kent Coast Electrification scheme and had a modified bogie to improve riding. *(Arthur Tayler)*

Close to Minster are the remains of Richborough Castle. It was a major port of Roman Britain later transformed into a civilian town. To supplement the harbour at Dover during WW1, Richborough was the prototype for sea-going Roll-on/Roll-off ferries to transport rolling stock, artillery and supplies to the Front. Attempts were made to develop the port after the war, especially for the transhipment of coal from the East Kent Rail, but little came of this. Part of the East Kent Railway operates as a heritage line between Shepherdswell (on the Dover–Faversham line) and Eythorne and is notable for being a centre of ex-SR and BR (Southern) electric multiple units. *(Simon Jeffs)*

Sandwich

It is thought to be where the Sandwich was invented by John Montagu, 4th Earl of Sandwich in the nineteenth century. There is a small village, Ham, nearby! Above: sandwich station. *('GB')*

STURRY

A telegraph station. HOTEL – The Swan.

OMNIBUSES to and from the station; also to Herne Bay, thrice daily,

Canterbury, etc. FAIR – Whit-Monday. MONEY ORDER OFFICE at Canterbury.

GROVE FERRY

A telegraph station. MONEY ORDER OFFICE at Canterbury.

From Sturry the main line proceeds in an east-north-east direction, through a highly cultivated country, and enters the Isle of Thanet, near Grove Ferry, where the railway crosses the Wausum, and proceeding five miles further, reaches the Minster Junction station, whence a branch line diverges to the ancient towns of Sandwich, and Deal, which we will describe first, and the other, the main line, proceeds to Ramsgate and Margate.

MINSTER JUNCTION

Distance from station, ¼ mile. A telegraph station.

OMNIBUSES to and from the station; also to Canterbury, *via* Monkton.

FAIR – Palm Monday. MONEY ORDER OFFICE at Ramsgate or Sandwich.

Many of our readers may not be aware that this spot, and the whole neighbourhood, is the classic ground of England, and replete with historical associations of surpassing interest. From the Downs to the north of the village of Minster there is a prospect of great extent and singular beauty. Not only may the Isle of Thanet, with all its churches save one, be seen at a glance, but in the distance are perceptible the towers of Reculver, the Isle of Sheppey, the Downs and town of Deal, the bay and town of Sandwich, the champaign districts of East Kent, the spires of Woodnesborough and Ash, the ruins of Richborough, the green levels of Minster and Saltpans, watered by the Stour, and far on the land horizon at the head of the valley the stately towers of Canterbury Cathedral, the picture finishing with a sweep of hills which spread north and south to the extent of one hundred miles.

Minster is a delightful looking village, and exceedingly interesting. The fine old church is said to be the oldest Christian church in England. The interior has been recently restored, and is very beautiful.

DEAL BRANCH

After leaving Minster, the line crosses the Stour by a double swing bridge built on a new and ingenious principle. Each line has its bridge; one turns to the right, and the other to the left, from a pivot on the side of the Ash, which is the next parish. By this arrangement greater stability is obtained, with a nicer power of adjustment. This bridge is considered an oddity by engineers, and it will well repay examination. It far surpasses the celebrated bridge at Norwich.

The line then proceeds over Sandwich flats past the hamlet of Saltpans. At this spot the memorable ruins of Richborough come fully into sight; and shortly after the train sweeps round the sandy hill on which they stand. This was a celebrated Roman station, which guarded the southern entrance of the great Roman haven, the area of which is now in the hands of agriculturalists and *'Corn now waves where Caesars once bore sway'.* The remains of a Roman amphitheatre are still quite apparent. In the centre of the great quadrangle is the celebrated prostrate cross, built to commemorate the introduction of Christianity into England. It is placed on the top of an immense heathen altar, and marks the spot on which Augustin preached the gospel. No monument in the kingdom equals that simple cross in interest, yet few have been treated with greater neglect. We commend it to the care of the clergy of Canterbury, the successors of Augustin and his eighty monks.

A short distance further, or four miles and a half from Minster, is the station of

SANDWICH

POPULATION, 2,944. A telegraph station. HOTEL – The Bell.
MARKET DAYS – Wednesdays (corn); alternate Mondays (cattle). FAIR –
December 4th. MONEY ORDER OFFICE at Sandwich.
BANKERS – The London and County Bank. Sub-Branch of National Provincial
Bank of England.

The traveller, on entering this place, beholds himself in a sort of Kentish Herculaneum, a town of the martial dead. He gazes around him, and looks upon the streets and edifices of a bye-gone age. He stares up at the beetling stories of the old pent-up buildings as he walks, and peers curiously through latticed windows into the vast low-roofed, heavy-beamed, oak-panelled rooms of days he has read of in old plays.

Deal, Walmer Castle and Sandown Castle

Its closeness to the notorious Goodwin Sands has made Deal a naturally sheltered anchorage allowing the town to become a significant port despite the absence of a harbour. Sandown, Deal and Walmer castles were constructed around the town by Henry VIII to protect against foreign naval attack, while several army barracks became established in the town around the time of the French Revolution. The Royal Marines were particularly associated with Deal, the Royal Marines School of Music not leaving until 1996 when the Deal barracks finally closed. The SER line from Minster reached Deal in 1847 but was not extended to Dover until 1881 which gives a clue to the remoteness of the area south of the town.

SANDWICH is a town of very remote antiquity, and contains more old buildings than almost any other in England. It is rich in ancient hospitals, chantries, hermitages and venerable churches, many of which, with their towers and buttresses, will take the imagination of the gazer back to the old monkish times, when Sandwich was the theatre of more stirring and important historical events than perhaps any town or port on our island.

Seven miles beyond Sandwich, the train reaches the terminus at

DEAL

POPULATION – 7,531. Distance from station, ½ mile. A telegraph station.
HOTEL – Royal. MARKET DAY – Saturday. FAIRS – April 5th and October 10th.
MONEY ORDER OFFICE at Deal.
BANKERS – Branch of the National provincial Bank of England.

This town stands close to the sea shore, which is a bold and open beach, being defended from the violence of the waves by an extensive sea wall of stones and pebbles which the sea has thrown up. The sea opposite the town between the shore and Goodwin Sands is termed the Downs. This channel is about eight miles long and six broad, and is a safe anchorage; and in particular quarters of the wind, as many as 400 ships can ride at anchor here at one time. Deal was formerly a rough-looking, irregular, sailor-like place, full of narrow streets, with shops, of multifarious articles termed slops or marine stores. It is however being much improved, and is now resorted to for sea bathing, especially on account of its good repute for moderate charges. The bathing establishment at Deal is well conducted, and there are good libraries.

It is a great pilot station for the licensed or branch pilots of the Cinque Ports; the Deal boatmen are as fine, noble and intrepid a race of seamen as any in the world, and as honest as they are brave. *Deal Castle* is at the south end of the town. The village of Walmer is a detached suburb of Deal, towards the south on the Dover Road. Since Her Majesty resided here, *Walmer* has been much improved and extended. It now contains several hundred handsome villas, inhabited by a large body of gentry. The air is very salubrious, and the surrounding country pleasant and agreeable.

Walmer Castle, one of the fortresses built by Henry in 1539, is the official residence of the Lord Warden of the Cinque Ports. It is surrounded by a moat and drawbridge. The apartments are small but convenient, and command a splendid view of the sea; but they will always have a peculiar interest for Englishmen, as having been the residence of the Duke of Wellington, and at which he died in 1852. *Sandown Castle* is about a mile to the north of Deal; it consists of a large central round tower, and four round bastions with port holes, and on the sea-side it is strengthened with an additional battery.

From Minster to Ramsgate the line is on a tolerably steep incline. Kent and the Kentish coast have long been celebrated for their delicious climate and exquisite

Ramsgate, Broadstairs and Margate

The three major resorts of the Isle of Thanet, the most easterly part of Kent, are to be considered as a whole to understand their complex history, particularly their railways. Ramsgate began as a fishing and farming hamlet and was a member of the Confederation of Cinque Ports, under the 'Limb' of Sandwich. By 1850, Ramsgate Harbour was completed and became a chief embarkation point both during the Napoleonic Wars and for the Dunkirk evacuation in 1940. Now the port has one of the largest marinas on the south coast and has provided cross-channel ferry services for many years. What Ramsgate, Margate and Broadstairs are really known for are their fine sandy beaches and the tourist industry that developed around them from the late eighteenth century. The area became a magnet for both the SER and LCDR, both companies developing separate stations in both Ramsgate and Margate. Ramsgate Town was reached by the SER in 1846 from Canterbury while its branch to Margate Sands station was opened 1863.

From the west came the LCDR, providing its own station at Margate (Margate West) in 1863 then on through Broadstairs to emerge right on the foreshore of the harbour at Ramsgate, named, appropriately enough, Ramsgate Harbour, *shown opposite*. It took the Southern Railway to sort this out in 1926. *Above:* Broadstairs station. *('GB')*

pastoral scenery, and the railway passes through a fine panorama of marine and picturesque views, until it reaches

RAMSGATE

POPULATION, 11,865. A telegraph station. HOTELS – Royal; Royal Albion; Royal Oak. MARKET DAYS – Wednesday and Saturday.
FAIRS – August 10th, at St Lawrence. MONEY ORDER OFFICE at Ramsgate.
BANKERS – Branch of the National Provincial Bank of England, Burgess and Son.

RAMSGATE was little better than a mere fishing village before the close of the last century, and all the noble streets and terraces stretching seaward are the growth of the present. Its prosperity has been literally built on a sandy foundation, more permanent than the adage would teach us to believe, for the sands, which are really unequalled for extent, were long the prominent attraction of visitors. In 1759 was commenced the pier, built chiefly of stone from the Purbeck and Portland quarries, involving an expenditure of nearly £600,000. This stupendous structure affords an excellent marine promenade of nearly 3,000 feet in length. The form is that of a polygon, with the two extremities about 200 feet apart. The harbour comprises an area of nearly fifty acres, and can receive vessels 500 tons at any state of the tide. The first object that arrests attention at the entrance is the obelisk, fifty feet in height, which commemorates the embarkation of George IV from here on his Hanoverian excursion in 1821. The next is a tablet, at the octagonal head, setting forth the name of the engineer and the dates of the erection. Opposite is the lighthouse, casting at night a brilliant reflection over the dark waste of waters, and forming a striking feature in the scenery of the coast. Far away, like a phosphoric gleam upon the channel, is the floating beacon called 'the Gull', which, with two smaller ones near Deal, becomes visible after dusk from the pier. Eight seamen and

Ramsgate Town and Harbour station were closed and replaced by a new station and a new line built to link the SER and LCDR route through Broadstairs to Margate, where, after the closure of the SER branch, all services were concentrated on an enlarged version of the former LCDR station, now plain Margate. *('GB', Peter de Russett)*

a captain, who has only occasionally a month's leave of absence, are entrusted with the management of the beacon, and in this desolate and dangerous region they are doomed to battle with the elements in all seasons, cheered alone by the reflection that through their vigilance thousands are perhaps annually preserved from the perils of shipwreck. The Goodwin Sands, traditionally said to have been the estate of Earl Godwin, father of King Harold, form the roadstead called the Downs, and extend from the North Foreland to Deal, but as they are continually shifting under the influence of the winds and the waves, their exact locality can never be ensured.

Nowhere is the accommodation for bathers more perfect than at Ramsgate, whether the green bosom of the Channel be selected for a plunge, or a private bath chosen instead. Most of these establishments where baths can be had at all hours, are elegantly fitted up with hot air stoves, luxuriant ottomans, and refectories and reading-rooms adjacent. A communication with the upper portions of the town, built upon the high range of cliffs, is formed by two convenient flights of stone steps called Augusta Stairs and Jacob's Ladder. The lawny esplanade that has been formed before the crescents facing the sea enables a promenader to obtain an ample sea view, and the Downs being continually studded with shipping, the picture is generally varied and animated. Some elegant churches in the florid Gothic style, and numerous places of dissenting worship, are to be met with in convenient situations about the town, and in harbour-street is the new Town Hall, erected in 1839, with a capacious market underneath, teeming with every kind of comestible of various degrees of excellence.

Boarding-houses, hotels and dining-rooms are in the usual watering-place abundance, and the limits of expenditure may be adjusted to the depth of every purse. The bazaars and libraries provide evening amusement through the agency of music and raffles; and though the books partake of the elderly Minerva press school of composition, and the raffling is generally for articles of indifferent worth, the excitement attendant upon both is quite sufficient for sea-side denizens.

No one of course would think of stopping a week at Ramsgate without going to Pegwell Bay, where the savoury shrimps and country-made brown bread and butter are supposed to have been brought to the very highest degree of perfection. And for a quiet stroll in another direction there is Broadstairs, two miles to the north-east, very genteel and very dull; the aspect of this 'exceedingly select' place of residence being so imposingly quiet as to make one involuntarily walk about on tip-toe for fear of violating the solemn sanctity of the place. It is, however, a very agreeable excursion for a day, and an excellent plan is to go by the path across the cliffs, past the elegant mansion of Sir Moses Montefiore, and return by the sands at low water. The old arch of York gate, built by the Culmer family in the reign of Henry VIII, is the sole vestige of the once extensive fortifications that bristled up at the back of the old quay. There was pier, too, swept away by the terrific storm in 1808, which destroyed that of Margate, but the rough wooden substitute is not the less picturesque, and there is a fine wholesome odour of sea-weed about the old rugged rafters, enough to make one willing to forego the fashionable for the fragrant. A mile beyond is Kingsgate, where Charles II landed, and furnished a pretext for endowing it with a regal title. Another mile, and the North Foreland lighthouse, 63 feet in height, may be reached and entered too, if the curious visitor will disburse a small gratuity to the keeper. It is well worthy of inspection.

Four miles distant from Ramsgate, the traveller reaches the terminus at

MARGATE

POPULATION, 8,874. Distance from station, ½ mile. A telegraph station. HOTELS – Gardiner's Royal; White Hart. STEAMERS to London daily in summer, thrice weekly in winter. MARKET DAYS – Wednesday and Saturday. MONEY ORDER OFFICE at Margate. BANKERS – Cobb & Co.

There is not, in the whole range of our sea-side physiology, a more lively, bustling place than this said Margate: albeit, by those who are fettered down to cold formalities, and regard laughter as a positive breach of good-breeding, it is pronounced to be essentially and irredeemably vulgar. The streets are always a scene of continued excitement, and troops of roguish, ruddy-cheeked urchins, escorted by their mammas and nursery maids, traverse every thoroughfare about the town from morning till night. There is a theatre also, and a kind of minor Vauxhall, called the *Tivoli*, where those who care little for out-of-door enjoyments can spend a passable hour in such dramatic and musical gratifications as the artists and the place can best afford. Bazaars and marine libraries afford too, in 'the season', the latest metropolitan vocal novelties; and the same raffling and rattling of dice boxes, to test fortune's favouritism, is carried on as at Ramsgate, but with a greater spirit of freedom and earnestness. In short, for those who do not go to the coast for retirement, and who like to have an atmosphere of London life surrounding them at the sea-side, there is no place where their desires can be so easily and comprehensively gratified as here.

The increasing extent and importance of the town makes one regard the traditions told of its early origin as being nearly akin to the fabulous, yet a few centuries back, known to the local chroniclers as coeval with the period of 'once-upon-a-time', Margate was a small fishing village, with a few rude huts thrown up along the beach, and having a *mere* or stream flowing at that point into the sea, whence it derived its present appellation. When London folks, however, grew wiser, and found that short trips had a wonderful power in preventing long doctor's bills, the place grew rapidly into repute, and the old Margate hoy – immortalised by Peter Pindar – disgorged its hundreds of buff-slippered passengers annually. Since then steam has done wonders, and Margate's visitors have to be numbered by hundreds of thousands in the space of time. The only drawback to its salubrity as a place of residence is that a cold cutting north-easterly wind is frequently encountered, and not being sheltered by a range of hills, the effect of the invalid of delicate constitution is of rather an injurious tendency than otherwise. But this apart, the air is keen, fresh, and invigorating, and, with persons in good health, will have a material influence in keeping them so. It is generally a few degrees cooler in July and August than Ramsgate.

The sixth day of April, 1810, saw the commencement of the present pier, and five years afterwards it was finished from a design by Rennie, and at a cost of £100,000. It is 900 feet in length, 60 feet wide, and 26 feet high. A day ticket for one penny will not only give admission to the promenade, but afford an opportunity besides of hearing a band perform for a few hours in the evening. There is a lighthouse at the extremity, which is an elegant ornamental Doric column as well, and was erected in 1829. At an expenditure of £8,000 the well-known Jarvis Jetty was constructed in 1824, out of the finest old English oak that could be procured. It extends 1,120 feet from the shore, and forms a pleasant cool promenade when the tide is out, although a scurrilous wag has compared it to walking along an excessively attenuated cold gridiron. The Clifton Baths, by the Fort, cut out of the chalk cliffs, are unquestionably the most commodious, and have some interesting appendages in the shape of a library, winding passages, curious vaults, daily newspapers and an organ. The other bathing-houses, though well conducted, are of a more ordinary character.

Margate being situated partly on the acclivities of two hills, and partly in the valley below, the streets partake of that tortuous and undulating character which is so much pleasanter to look at than to climb. On the Fort, in front of East-crescent, the structure of Trinity Church is conspicuously situated, and to the south-east the old parish church of St John occupies a similarly elevated position. In this latter there are some curious old tombs and monumental brasses and should not be forgotten. A literary and scientific institution is supported by the annual subscriptions of the inhabitants, and has a library, reading room and museum, that may vie with any out of London.

Extending about a mile along the shore there is a stout barricade of stone, erected as a defence to the incursions of the sea, at an outlay of £20,000. The sum of £4,000 more rebuilt the Town Hall and market Place in 1821; and from this it will be seen the townsfolk have not been chary of their coin in contributing to the security and embellishment of their native place. Inns and hotels of every grade are scattered in and about the town with prodigal luxuriance, and lodging-houses are everywhere. The staple manufacture of the landladies here may be set down as – beds.

The visitor should not neglect to make a pilgrimage to the old Roman station of Reculver and Richborough, the ruins of the old castle of the latter being in a state of tolerable preservation. Races are held on the downs, by Dandelion, in the middle of September, and generally attract a large concourse of spectators.

HASTINGS BRANCH

Ashford to Hastings

HAM STREET and APPLEDORE stations.

RYE

POULATION, 8,202. A telegraph station. HOTEL – George.
OMNIBUSES to Peasmarsh, Beckley, Northiam, Newenden, Rolvenden, and Benenden.
MARKET DAYS – Wednesday (Corn), Saturday (Meal) and every Wednesday fortnight (stock). FAIRS – Whit-Monday and August 10th.
MONEY ORDER OFFICE. BANKERS – Curteis, Pomfret, Pix, Billingham and Pix. Branch of London and County Bank.

Rye

Quite simply, Rye is one of the most beautiful towns in England. It has a long seafaring history, legally as one of the two 'Antient Townes' (Winchelsea being the other). Rye was to become a limb of the Cinque Ports Confederation by 1189, and subsequently a full member, illegally, being involved with smuggling gangs of the eighteenth and nineteenth centuries, who used such inns as the 1156-vintage Mermaid Inn and The Olde Bell Inn, connected by a secret passage way. Such historic roots and charm make Rye a major tourist destination, although fishing and shipping are still important.

Above and left: Sited on a hill, crowned by its church, Rye is visible from the surrounding flatlands, formerly marsh reclaimed from the sea. The SER line from Ashford opened in October 1850 and from Hastings in February 1851. Despite several attempts to close the line, it still retains an hourly service that runs from Brighton to Ashford, allowing connection with Eurostar services. The well-proportioned original station building is still in use. *(Fred Matthews)*

RYE, a borough town in the county of Sussex. It stands on an eminence near the mouth of the river Rother. In the reign of Edward III, Rye sent nine armed vessels to the royal fleet when that monarch invaded France. In the next reign it was burnt and plundered by the French. From this and other unfavourable circumstances, the town remained for many years in a state of decay, but its prosperity has in great measure been restored.

WINCHELSEA

Distance from station, 1½ miles. A telegraph station. HOTEL – New Inn.

PASSENGER VANS to Hastings. MARKET DAY – Saturday. FAIR – May 14th (Cattle).

MONEY ORDER OFFICE.

The original sea port, which bore its name, was swallowed up by the sea, and although the buildings were then erected further inland, unappeased by the former sacrifice, broke in anew, and finally, in the time of Queen Elizabeth, altogether choked up the harbour. The ruins of the castle of Ounber, built by Henry VIII, are still standing, and so are three out of the four town gates, but they are in ruinous condition.

HASTINGS

Descriptive particulars of this place will be found earlier.

South Eastern Main Line continued

Ashford to Folkestone and Dover

The main line on leaving Ashford makes a gradual approach towards the coast, swerving slightly to the south-east, and having on each side a delightful champaign country. At one part of the route the vestiges of a celebrated fortress suddenly burst upon the vision through the trees to the right, forming all that remains of *Westhanger Castle*.

The second object worthy of notice is

Merstham Hatch, the property of the Knatchbull family since the reign of Henry VII. The mansion is a modern building, of considerable architectural beauty, situated in a very fine park, and the interior is most elegantly fitted up.

Mount Morris, the seat of Lord Rokeby, is in a splendid park, the heights of which command extensive views of the South Downs, the Channel, and the coast of France.

From this point the passes almost immediately to the north of the extensive level of Romney Marsh, which may occasionally be seen from the carriages.

WESTENHANGER

Distance from station, ½ mile. A telegraph station.

MONEY ORDER OFFICES at Folkestone and Ashford.

Winchelsea today is a new town – the original was swallowed up by the waves in 1287. Once a port, the sea is now several miles away and the tiny town, with three of its four medieval gates still intact, is considered the smallest town in England. A quiet, peaceful place with a large church, the station is over a mile away down a very steep hill and, subsequently, is little used. *(Laurel Arnison)*

Hythe is somewhat of an oddity in this book. A Cinque Port, it did not get a railway link until 1874 from Sandling Junction, and this only lasted until 1951 due to its inconvenient position high above the town. Since 1927, it has been the terminus of the 'Smallest Public Railway in the World', the 15-inch gauge Romney, Hythe & Dymchurch Railway which runs along the coast to Dungeness, a distance of 13½ miles. Well worth a visit. *(Simon Jeffs)*

The SER arrived in the Folkestone in June 1843 on its way to Dover. The difficult terrain necessitated the building of a nineteen-arch viaduct at Foord to Folkestone Junction, where the line to the harbour station branched off. The harbour had been developed by the SER and became the main embarkation point for that company's ferry services to Boulogne. *('GB')*

Two and a half miles from here are the ruins of *Westhanger Castle*, once the abode of the ill-fated fair Rosamond, which are well worthy a visit from any person staying in the neighbourhood.

HYTHE

HOTEL – White Hart. A telegraph station

HYTHE lies 3½ miles to the south of Westenhanger station, easily accessible by omnibuses that meet the trains.

The town of Hythe is small, but clean and healthy, and prettily situated at the foot of a hill extending down to the sea. It is beginning to be resorted to by visitors, for whom accommodation is provided at reasonable terms. The church on the hill has a light tower, ornamented by four turrets. It is one of the Cinque ports. Near Hythe commences Romney Marsh, extending along the coast for twenty miles and including about 60,000 acres, which within the last few years have been successfully drained and cultivated.

The deep chalk cutting that succeeds our departure from Westenhanger introduces us to Saltwood Tunnel, and, emerging from this, we immediately catch on the right the first transient glimpse of the sea – that sight which involuntarily quickens our pulse, and sends a pleasurable emotion tingling through our veins. A lofty amphitheatre of hills, stretching away in the blue distance, varies the view in the opposite direction. Then comes an embankment, and borne across a viaduct 90 feet above the valley, we come almost magically within a fine view of Folkestone and its harbour, immediately afterwards reaching the station at

FOLKESTONE

POPULATION, 8,507. A telegraph station.
HOTELS – Pavilion; Royal George; Clarendon.
OMNIBUSES to and from the station; also to Sandgate, Ashford, Canterbury, etc.
POST HORSES, FLYS etc., at the hotels. STEAMERS – to Boulogne, twice daily in the summer, in two hours, and once in the winter.
MARKET DAY – Thursday. FAIRS – June 28th and Thursday in Easter Week.
MONEY ORDER OFFICE.
BANKERS – Branch of the National Provincial Bank of England.

FOLKESTONE is rapidly becoming a much frequented watering place, as well as a favourite point of embarkation to France; the distance to Boulogne is only 27 miles, and the voyage generally accomplished in two hours and a half. The opening of the South Eastern Railway, and the establishment of a line of packets between this port and Boulogne, has been the means of recuing Folkestone from its previous obscurity, and bringing it to its present position. It is situated on the side of a range of hills on very uneven ground, the streets are narrow, steep and irregular, and the sea-worn chasms about the shore seem still to perpetuate in appearance that reputation for contraband traffic which once was its distinguishing feature. The air is very salubrious, and has been though of much efficacy in nervous debility, while the country round is highly picturesque, and abounds in varied and beautiful landscapes. Visitors here may enjoy

Dover

Both the SER and LCDR aimed for the town, the latter carving through the chalk at Abbotscliffe and Shakespeare tunnels to arrive at the port in February 1844.

The LCDR arrived from Canterbury in 1861, their trains terminating at Dover Priory station for a short while until the line to Dover Harbour station in the Western Docks area was completed. SER trains served Dover Town for a while, but both companies eventually extended their boat trains onto the Admiralty Pier. The exposed halt here was replaced by a covered station, Dover Marine (later, Dover Western Docks), available to passengers in 1919. It closed in 1994 with the demise of boat trains and the opening of the Tunnel, it is now a cruise liner terminal. Trains in Dover now use Dover Priory. *(Chris Wilson)*

all the benefits of sea bathing and sea air, with more retirement than at Dover and Ramsgate.

Folkestone Hill is 575 feet high and commands a beautiful prospect of the town and adjacent country, through which the railway is seen winding its devious course. To those who do not mind a little pedestrianism, and who delight in formidable ascents and footpaths trembling on the brink of ocean, we can conscientiously recommend a walk across the cliffs at Dover, which beside presenting a succession of romantic scenery will be found to afford some advantageous opportunities for inspecting the shafts connected with the ventilation of the railway tunnels running underneath.

Sandgate, a small watering place two miles from Folkestone, has been much frequented within the last twenty years by invalids, who wish for quiet and retirement. It has several detached villas, and the roads between Folkestone and Sandgate, either along the shore or over the cliff, are exceedingly picturesque and romantic. *Sandgate Castle* is of great antiquity. The country around is highly interesting, and abounds in beautiful views and landscapes, ruined castles and other remains of olden times.

After leaving Folkestone, the traveller will encounter the most wonderful portion of the line. The rapidity of our progress is such as to allow but little time, however, for examination of the extraordinary engineering works and achievements. Prepared by a shrill shriek of the whistle, we plunge into the Martello tunnel, and then, scarcely with a breathing interval, enter the second or Abbot's Cliff tunnel. Emerging from this, the line continues along a terrace supported by a sea wall for nearly a mile, and presenting a delicious scenic contrast with the marine expanse that opens to the right. This brings us to the Shakespeare Cliff tunnel, double arched for greater security, on escaping from which, an embankment raised from the shingle again receives us, and darting through the smaller excavation of Arch-cliff Fort, we are brought, with varied sensations of dreamy wonder and delight, beneath the elegant terminus at Dover.

The viaduct on the Dover side is also considered a fine work; it is about half a mile long, and formed of heavy beams of timber securely framed and bolted together, but left open so as to offer less resistance to the waves in bad weather.

DOVER

POULATION, 25,325. A telegraph station. HOTELS – The Ship; The Lord Warden; The Gun. POST HORSES, FLYS, etc., at the hotels.
BOATS to mail packets when outside harbour, fare, 2s each person.
PORTERAGE of luggage to packets and station, 1s to 1s 6d each person.
COACH to Walmer and Deal, four times daily. STEAMERS to Calais, Boulogne and Ostend, daily, except on Sundays. MARKET DAYS – Wednesday and Saturday.
FAIRS – November 23rd, lasting over three market days, and Charlton Fair in July.
MONEY ORDER OFFICE, Dover. BANKERS – National Provincial Bank of England.

This much frequented point of continual embarkation has of late years occupied a prominent position among the watering-places of our island. The line of continuous

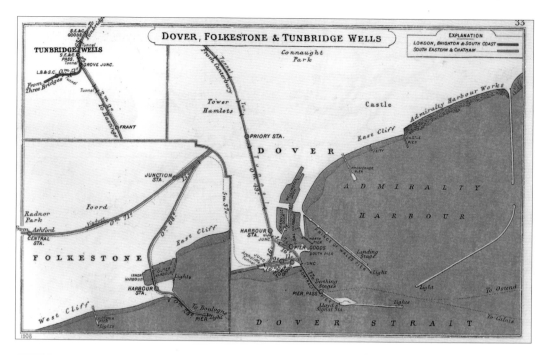

DOVER, FOLKESTONE & TUNBRIDGE WELLS

Above: Railway map, *c.* 1910.

Left and below: The harbour station and branch opened in 1847, surviving until March 2009 when the last train arrived. Formal closure notices have been issued for the branch which is currently derelict. The northern suburb of Cheriton, on the line to Dover and the M20 motorway is the site of the English terminal of the Channel Tunnel. *(Robert Armstrong)*

Construction of the Channel Tunnel began in 1988 and it opened in 1994. The passenger terminal is wedged between the Downs and the M20 motorway just west of Castle Hill, while freight trains are marshalled at Dollands Moor Freight Yard further west. *(SEG archives)*

terraces of noble-looking mansions spreading along the margin of the coast, the pureness of its atmosphere, the bold and rocky headlands that distinguish its marine scenery, all contribute to give it an important position among the recently created destinations of our sea-loving citizens. The associations, too, that cling to the white cliffs of Albion – not, as of yore, frowning defiance to our Gallic neighbours, but with a better spirit illuminating their weather-beaten features with sunny smiles of welcome – all tend to draw every year crowds of fleeting visitors to a spot so renowned in song and story. It has been well said, that scarcely any giant man, from King Arthur to Prince Albert, has failed, at some period or other, to visit Dover, and all history confirms the assertion.

Divided from the French coast by a passage of only twenty miles across the British Channel, Dover is advantageously situated on the margin of a picturesque bay, sheltered by the promontory of the South Foreland, and screened by its lofty cliffs from the piercing northerly winds.

At the entrance to the town from London-road was the Hospital of St Mary, commonly called the *Maison Dieu*, and now the guildhall and gaol. It was erected in the reign of King John, by Hubert de Burgh (afterwards Earl of Kent), and intended for the accommodation of pilgrims passing through Dover on their way to or from the Continent. After many changes and alterations, as well as being fortified during the civil war, it was purchased from Government by the corporation in 1834, and converted the following year into a guildhall, sessions chamber and gaol. The old priory gate, half monastery, half farm, is still remaining, at the beginning of the carriage road towards Folkestone.

Over the butter market in the London-road was the old Town Hall, erected in the reign of James I, on the site of an ancient cross. It is now the Dover Museum, and may be inspected daily from ten till five by the public. The collection comprises various specimens of birds, reptiles, fishes, insects, minerals, fossils, weapons, dresses, coins and other articles illustrative of the manners and customs of different nations.

Under the museum, the butter market presents, on a Saturday, a busy and lively scene, and the commodities that then pour in from every part of the surrounding country are both plentiful and excellent.

Ancient as Dover is as a town and port, it is, as we have said, comparatively modern as a watering-place. In 1817, houses were commenced on the Marine Parade, and about the same period, Liverpool Terrace, and the contiguous lawns, Guildford and Clarence, were projected, followed, in 1838, by the noble mansions of Waterloo Crescent and the Esplanade. These form, in conjunction with others, a continuous range of imposing buildings that extend nearly from the castle cliff to the north pier. Close to the sea is the Promenade, which, during the summer season, presents a complete galaxy of beauty and fashion, not unfrequently enlivened by the performance of military music. The facilities afforded to bathers merit great commendation, and the clear transparency of the water is not the least of the advantages here derived.

If not the most elegant thoroughfare in Dover, Snargate Street is decidedly the most picturesque. With the towering white cliffs on one side, and a row of excellent shops on the other, it presents a contrast that seems to link agreeably the permanent majesty of the past with the fleeting characteristics of the present. Here is situated the Post Office, nearly opposite to Rigden's library, the theatre, the Apollonian Hall in which concerts are frequently given, and a bazaar, which affords a pleasant lounge for those who like to court the smiles of fortune in a raffle. Adjoining the Wesleyan Chapel, also in the same street, is the entrance to the grand military shaft leading to the heights and barracks above. The communication is by an arched passage and a vertical excavation having three spiral flights of 140 steps each. The barracks are sufficiently capacious to contain many thousand troops; and beyond, following the military road, we come to the grand redoubt, occupying the site of an ancient Pharos, the ruins of which are called Bredenstone, or the 'Devil's Drop'. Nowhere will the tourist find more extensive and beautiful views than a promenade at sunset on these heights will afford. Westward is the town of Boulogne, with its lofty column to commemorate an invasion which never took place; eastward, rising as it were from the ocean, is the white tower of the Hotel de Ville, and the revolving phare of the town of Calais. Turn which way we will there is something to admire. On one side is the magnificent castle, still rearing its stately battlements in majestic grandeur, after braving the blasts of a thousand winters, and bringing back to the eye of the imaginative beholder the by-past glories of the days of chivalry; on the other, the noble cliff, an object sufficiently striking from its own native sublimity, but rendered doubly attractive and interesting to every spectator by its association with the greatest work of our greatest bard. Perhaps in the whole circuit of the kingdom there is not another spot so calculated to awaken in the bosom of

At last we arrive in Dover, where people have entered and left Britain since prehistory. It faces France, twenty-one miles away, across the Straits of Dover and is flanked by the famous White Cliffs of Dover of wartime memory. One of the UK's major ports, with very frequent ferry services to France and Belgium, a major military centre based on Dover Castle and on the front line of every threat that England has faced from invaders, Dover is steeped in history. (Simon Jeffs)

an Englishman feelings of pride and exultation, as the objects around call up in succession reminiscences of those martial and intellectual achievements by which the inviolate island of the sage and free has attained her present unquestioned supremacy among the nations of the world. An evening stroll will amply repay the trouble of the ascent.

Shakespeare's Cliff is about one mile west of the pier, and is exactly 313 feet above high-water mark, being somewhat less than it was in the days of our great dramatist. The descriptive passage that has stood sponsor to it has been so often quoted that we may be well spared its repetition here. A steady foot and a cool head will enable a visitor himself to learn from experience 'how fearful and dizzy 'tis to cast one's eyes so low'.

But the Castle is, after all, the great lion of Dover, and as the first object that strikes conspicuously upon the eye of the traveller as he emerges from the railway terminus, it is sure to woo his footsteps thither as the cynosure of attraction. Starting on his pilgrimage, early enough, if possible, to behold the artistic effect of the grey sombre ruins, magnified by contrast with a skiey background from which the shades of departing night have not altogether fled, we can promise the pedestrian a rare treat. A sunrise scene from the cliffs round the Castle will honestly challenge comparison with a sunset from the Alps. Well aware that this savours of a bold assertion not altogether orthodox, we merely recommend such as would doubt its veracity to ask Boots to call them at two o'clock in the morning and try it. Rising northward of the town, from a bold and abrupt ascent of more than 300 feet, and poised upon a commanding eminence, which seems to defy alike the ravages of time and war, Dover Castle answers more to our expectations of what a fortress ought to be than any other defensive building in the kingdom. Its early origin is involved in the mystery of a tradition, though there can be little doubt that a British fortification was the nucleus of its future architectural strength. Julius Caesar has had the honour of erecting the present fortress ascribed to him, but recent antiquaries have come to the conclusion that it was raised between the years Ad 43 and 49, during the reign of Claudius. The three leading characteristics of the ground plans and buildings are Roman, Saxon and Norman. All that can now be traced of the fortifications of the former is encircled by a deep ditch. The Saxon portion of the structure is presumed to have been commenced by Alfred the Great, and the foundation of the present keep to have originated with the ingenious Gundulph, Bishop of Rochester, about the year 1153. In its present state the Castle occupies about thirty-six acres.

On approaching the entrance to the castle from the old Deal road the stranger's notice is first attracted by the faint tinkle of a small bell, moved by a string from the tower of Fulbert de Dover, now used as a debtor's prison. A grated window fronts the road, at which a prisoner stations himself to solicit alms, aided by a further appeal on a board, which bears the following inscription:

Oh! Ye whose hours exempt from sorrow flow,
Behold the seat of pain, and want, and woe!
Think while your hands the entreated alms extend,
That what to us ye give to God ye lend.

It is seldom that an application of so mournful a nature can be neglectfully regarded. With a glance at the curious piece of brass ordnance, cast at Utrecht in 1544, and twenty-four

Advertising poster, *c.* 1910, for 'The Most interesting Town on the South Coast'. *(CMcC)*

feet in length, known as 'Queen Elizabeth's pocket pistol', we ascend the road leading to the keep, and pass through the gateway from Peverell's Tower, so denominated from an illegitimate son of the Conqueror, who had the command of this post. The keep, situated in the centre of the quadrangle, is the large square edifice rising 370 feet above the level of the sea, presenting from its summit a view of almost unequalled grandeur. The famous well, 400 feet deep, was once an important feature of the tower, but it is now arched over for better security of the public. The old Roman church, and the pharos, or lighthouse, adjoining, are the next objects of interest; its form is that of a cross, with a square tower. On the western side of the church is Cocklecrow or Colton's Gate. Some curious excavations have been made in more modern times for the reception of soldiers, about 2,000 of whom can be here conveniently accommodated; light and air are conveyed into the different apartments by circular apertures cut in the chalk, and by other openings carried through to the face of the cliffs. These remarkable subterranean barracks can be seen on Tuesdays and Fridays by an order from the commanding royal engineer, which can be easily obtained on those days between the hours of ten and twelve at the Ordnance Office, Archcliff Fort. Subterranean communications exist in every direction. Blanchard, the celebrated French aeronaut, ascended in 1785 from the quadrangle of the castle keep, and after a voyage of two hours and a half, descended in safety on the continent, at the distance of six miles from Calais. Our modern steam-boat communication has long since out-rivalled the aerial voyager in speed.